Praise for *Escape from Slavery*

"[*Escape from Slavery*] carries the uncalculating ring of truth."
—*San Francisco Chronicle*

"A chilling tale."
—Karen Hunter, New York *Daily News*

"How will the world respond to Francis Bok's true story? Some will welcome its commercial profitability and entertainment value. And some will seek to change the world."
—Anne Grant, *Providence Journal*

"This is a powerful, exceptionally well-told story, equally riveting and heartbreaking. Although legal strides have been made, with the help of people like Bok, the persistence of slavery in the world makes this a work that can't be ignored."
—*Publishers Weekly* (starred review)

"Bok's saga provides another—more contemporary—perspective on slavery for Americans reckoning with their own troubling history of such inhumanity."
—*Booklist*

ESCAPE
FROM
SLAVERY

ESCAPE
FROM
SLAVERY

The True Story of My Ten Years
in Captivity—and My Journey
to Freedom in America

FRANCIS BOK
WITH EDWARD TIVNAN

ST. MARTIN'S GRIFFIN 🌿 NEW YORK

Design by Phil Mazzone
Map by Paul J. Pugliese

www.stmartins.com

Library of Congress Cataloging-in-Publication Data

Bok, Francis.
    Escape from slavery : the true story of my ten years in
captivity—and my journey to freedom in America / Francis Bok,
with Edward Tivnan.
        p. cm.
    ISBN 0-312-30623-7 (hc)
    ISBN 0-312-30624-5 (pbk)
    EAN 978-0312-30624-3
    1. Bok, Francis. 2. Sudanese Americans—Biography.
3. Slaves—Sudan—Biography. 4. Slavery—Sudan. 5. Sudan—
Biography. I. Tivnan, Edward. II. Title.

E184.S77B65 2003
305.5'67'092—dc21
[B]
                                                    2003047132

10 9 8 7 6

For my mother, my two sisters, and my brother—but especially for my father, who always told me I would do something important in life. Also, for those who are still slaves and those who are fighting for freedom in Sudan.

CONTENTS

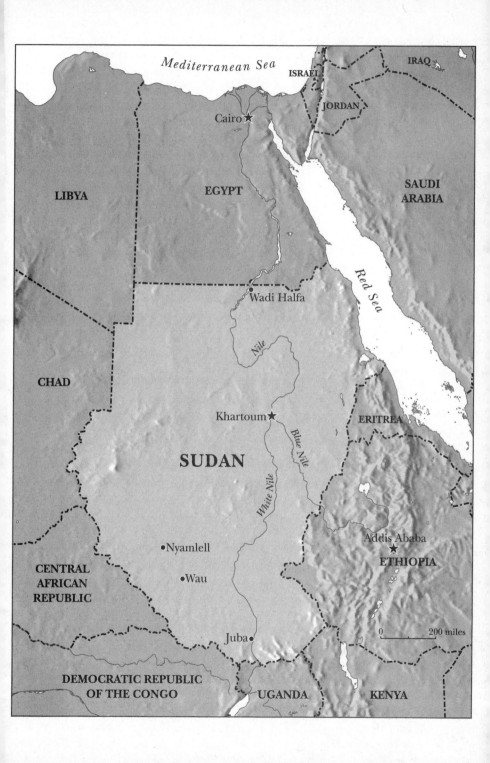

ESCAPE
FROM
SLAVERY

CHAPTER ONE

THE RAID

I have told the story many times about that day in 1986, when my mother sent me to the market to sell eggs and peanuts: the day I became a slave. But, as I begin to tell my story here, I realize that I have never before discussed how happy my life was just hours before it changed forever. Too many bad memories left no space for the good ones. Yet, before the misery, loneliness, and constant fear that my childhood became, before the ten years when my only friends were Giemma Abdullah's goats and cows, I remember my father's farm in southern Sudan, where every day seemed full of family, friends, and love. I was only seven years old in 1986, and now that I am in my twenties I have many questions about those days, which that little boy in far-off Africa cannot answer. But even as a mere seven-year-old, I was aware that my life was good and might get better.

It was not so for everyone in our village, and I felt sorry for the poor who lived there. Sometimes people would come to our farm to beg for milk and cheese. We had plenty of both; we had chickens, goats, sheep, and cows; we had beautiful green trees with ripe yellow mangoes that we could pick off and eat, and coconuts as big as your head. My family grew peanuts and other kinds of beans. We were surrounded by green fields of sorghum where I would play with my sisters, Amin, who was twelve, and baby Achol, who could barely walk. We lived in two large houses—one for the men, the other for the women—made from mud and topped by straw roofs shaped like upside down cones. Even the cattle had their own hut with a roof of straw to keep them warm in the winter and to protect them from the rain. Our farm was full of life—animals, plants, families—and there a little boy could do almost anything that he wanted.

I did not go to school. No one in my family had any formal education; I don't think I knew what a school was or what happened there. I had heard the word "school," but all it meant to me was a place that some kids from the village had been sent to in Juba, the capital city of southern Sudan, near the borders of Zaire and Uganda. In Gourion, my village, there was no school, and like most little Dinka boys, I spent my days in a pair of shorts, nothing but underwear really, no shirt, barefoot, playing with my sisters and friends.

We played *alweth*: We would run off and hide in the fields, leaving one of us to find the others. And when he found someone, he would chase them and try to touch them—hide-and-seek, Dinka style. We also had our own kind of baseball or cricket, called *madallah*. All we needed was a stick and a chunk of rubber the size of a hockey puck, made either from the heel of an old shoe or from an old car tire. Then we made teams—four on a side—and someone threw the puck and another hit it, and someone else tried to hit it back, as hard as possible. The point was to keep the rubber in the air. Whoever missed it, lost. Madallah is a game of energy and power, and I loved play-ing this game.

If I was lucky, my eighteen-year-old brother John—I called him by his Dinka name Buk—would let me watch him and his friends at their games. In the evening, when it was cooler, the big kids played *jeddi*. Ten boys, five to a side. Each boy would bend a leg at the knee and hold it by the ankle, jumping around on one leg within a big circle. The aim was to get one person on your side past the others by blocking and preventing them from pushing him over. My little friends and I also played jeddi. If we got a good game going, other kids would come to watch and want to play. That would increase the excitement of the game, and all of us would try even harder to impress the audience.

One of my favorite activities was making little cows. The Sudanese measure wealth in terms of how many cows you have, and little boys like me created our own herds out of the clay from the ground. My brother was very good at this, and he taught me how to take a handful of mud and sculpt it into a miniature cow. My friends and I spent hours sitting in the vil-lage under a tree making animals, sometimes goats and sheep, but mainly cows. Days passed unnoticed; in the morning I would begin molding the clay and suddenly it was time to go home to eat. Each of us made a shelter for our cattle, which we were allowed to leave right there in the village in a special place until the next sculpting session.

But what I liked to do most was follow my father around the farm. If he was digging in the fields, I began digging. If he was pulling sorghum grasses from the ground, I tried to pull them, too.

"Go play with your friends!" he would say. But I wanted to help my father, and he seemed to be pleased that I liked to work at his side. I felt my father's love every day. He had eight children, four older than this eager seven-year-old running in his shadow. But he always talked to me, encouraged me. He often would hug me and hoist me up on his shoulders and let me ride him on his visits to his friends in the village. "What do you want, Piol?" he asked me every night, and "What do you need, Piol?" every morning. That he had named me "Piol" was an honor. It was a favorite name in his family, the Dinka word for "rain." Francis was my Christian name, but in my village I was Piol Bol (my father's name) Buk (his father's name).

One day my father called me by a new name, *muycharko,* which means "twelve men." I asked him, "Why do you call me *muycharko?*"

He laughed at my question. Then he explained that out of all his children I was the one who wanted to work the hardest, the child who always got what he wanted, the one who would never give up.

"You are like twelve men," he said. "I think you will be a successful man. I think you will be able to do something important when you grow up."

I felt my father's words flow into my body and fill me with happiness. I had never heard my father say such a thing to any of his other children. My father thought I could be a great man, so I dreamed of being a great man with a big farm and many cattle.

I had heard people in the village refer to my father as *ajak,* which in the Dinka language means "rich man." We had hundreds and hundreds of cows, sheep, and goats. The story was that, to marry my mother he had to pay eighty cattle as a dowry to her family. He also had another wife for whom he paid more than a hundred cattle. We kept a hundred and fifty or so in the large hut near our houses, and a thousand head more grazed in the grasslands a long walk away from the family compound. (My father's other wife Marial and their four children lived nearby and tended his other herd. I visited them often and Marial was a second mother to me.)

My father often went to Juba to buy and sell livestock. He also had traveled to other countries in Africa, places with strange, beautiful names like Kenya and Uganda, where they did not speak the Dinka language. I, too, dreamed of traveling to those places—and others. I would be ajak like my father Bol Buk, who owned what seemed to me the best farm in Gourion, a village of the Dinka people near the River Lol, in the state of Aweil, in the Bahr al-Ghazal region of southwestern Sudan, about sixty miles south of what the maps call the Bahr al-Arab River (the Dinka call it the Kiir), the border between the north and south of Sudan.

When my mother told me that she had instructed the other kids in the village to bring me along on their trip to the nearby market town of Nyamlell, I saw it as the first step to becoming the important man my father thought I could be. This would not be my first visit to Nyamlell. My father had taken me to the Nyamlell market to trade animals and sorghum, and my mother often walked there on market days, balancing a huge tin of milk or cheese on her head. A few times she had brought me along to help her sell our extra milk and cheese and buy other things that the family needed.

Our family also attended a Catholic Church there, the same church I was baptized in. I never knew why my father was a Christian, or when he became one; perhaps his family had joined the church generations before, during the British colonial era in Sudan. Christian missionaries had been encouraged to travel through the south to help the people, and representatives of various denominations built churches and schools, preaching the gospel to the Dinka. Today, about twenty percent of the people of southern Sudan call themselves Christians, adopting the version of Christianity of the local missionaries who happened to move to their area. My parents were probably baptized into the Roman Catholic Church because the closest church to our village was the Catholic one in Nyamlell. I have no idea why they chose the name "Francis" for me, though I am now aware that there are several famous saints with that name. Our family did not go to services every week. Attending mass, I will confess, was not my favorite activity as a seven-year-old. I quickly got bored with the ceremony, and my father would let me leave to play outside with the other little kids.

On market day, Nyamlell was filled with people, a whirl of sounds and smells that did not exist on our farm. Nyamlell made my skin tingle. Today I would be on my own. I knew my mother was giving me a big honor, and I wanted to prove that she was right to trust me to sell her hard-cooked eggs and peanuts. I would show her—and my father—that I was a great trader in the making.

The other kids turned up, about ten of them, including my eleven-year-old friend Piol Kvol, and two twelve-year-old girls named Nyabol and Abuk, both of whom my mother trusted to supervise me. I was wearing my shirt to reflect my responsibility.

She handed Kvol the pole with two tins of eggs and peanuts attached to it and gave me my instructions.

"When you sell something," she warned, "give the money to the older children so you do not lose it." She also set the rules: The trip to Nyamlell was about business, not fooling around in the marketplace with new playmates. I must listen to the big girls, Nyabol and Abuk.

"Yes, yes," I said and grabbed the carrying pole from Kvol. They were my goods to sell, and if I was big enough to go to the market without my parents, I was strong enough to carry two tins of hard-cooked eggs and peanuts. I adjusted the pole to my shoulder for the right balance, and we set off on our adventure, the children from Gourion marching to Nyamlell on official business.

We walked toward the sun along a dusty road, across the river called Lol, and soon we could see on the hill up ahead the buildings and trees of Nyamlell. I adjusted my pole for the final stretch to the market where I would get a good price for my mother's eggs and peanuts. After all, I was Piol Bol Buk, also known as muycharko—"twelve men."

When we arrived at the marketplace, people were already set up under the shade of the trees and a dozen or so lean-tos made from burlap and sticks. It was still the dry season, when the sun is very hot in my country. The marketplace smelled rich—the fresh meat hanging by the stalls, the fish, the fruits, the vegetables, the fresh tobacco leaves on sale, all those odors mixed with the sweat of the people. (Every time I smell tobacco, I am back in Nyamlell on market day.) Flies buzzed around the meat and fish and pestered the little half-naked kids running around the area, laughing and pushing each other. But there was no playing for me, just selling. I was excited to get my trading career started.

The big kids picked a spot under a tree. It was late afternoon. In my country, we do not care about the time. No one had a watch. When the sun went down, it was time to go home. Even a seven-year-old knew that. There was plenty of light in the sky, and I had several hours ahead of me to sell my eggs and peanuts under the shady trees of Nyamlell. People approached the Gourion kids to check out our goods. They asked for prices, and when we told them, they tried to negotiate.

"Why are these eggs so expensive?" they complained. I did not know. Kvol and Nyabol had been told how much we could sell our food for, and they helped me make sure my customers did not get too much of a bargain.

The sun moved down in the sky. I made some sales, and gave the money to Kvol, just as my mother had said. I was selling more eggs than peanuts, but the people kept coming into the marketplace, hundreds of people, and I was sure they would buy all my food. Maybe I would also have time to play with the kids from the other villages who were running around the stalls.

Then something changed. People began walking faster, talking to each other rather than looking at the food. They seemed excited; some were pointing toward the river. I continued to sell my eggs and peanuts, but something was going on. I could not help listening to what the people were saying:

"Smoke" I heard, and "in the villages." Something had happened in the villages. The trees in the marketplace blocked our view of the river and plains below Nyamlell, but people now arrived from the part of town with a clear view of the villages to the west. What they saw worried them.

"There was big smoke," I heard someone say. All the children were listening, and more people came running into the market with news.

"Too much smoke for it to be only one house burning," one person said. Another added, "There was a storm of smoke rising from one village."

A storm of smoke? I wondered what that meant.

"Maybe the *murahaliin* came," I heard someone say. "They came and burned the houses." I was not sure what they meant. Murahaliin? I had heard people in my village talk of these "militia" from the north, dangerous men with guns who killed people and stole their cattle. There had been some kind of "war." But these were people I did not know, and I had never seen these murahaliin. I was seven years old, enjoying my first trip to the market on my own, selling my mother's hard-cooked eggs and peanuts.

But people had stopped buying. They were no longer looking at what we were selling. The adults understood what the others were talking about, the people who saw "the storm of smoke" rising from the direction we had just come from, from the village of Gourion, my village, where my family was.

The customers began to rush from the marketplace. The other sellers began gathering their things. Before the children from Gourion could decide what to do, we heard strange noises, bursts of loud sounds—tut-tut-tut-tut, tut-tut-tut-tut!

Suddenly, everyone was running in every direction. "The murahaliin are coming!" And wherever the people scattered, they ran into men with guns entering the marketplace. First men on horses, shooting people with bursts of fire and smoke from their rifles. Then men on foot, running and shooting and slashing at people with their long knives. Not ten men, not twenty, but many more, more than I knew how to count, maybe hundreds of men riding and running into the market-place, shooting and hacking people to the ground with their swords.

They were not Dinka people, but those my father had called "*Juur.*" I had seen them in the market before, black men, but with lighter skin than ours, in their headdresses and robes, who came from the north on camels loaded with the important things we do not have in southern Sudan—salt, sugar, tea. I had also heard people call these men (I had yet to see one of their women) *djellabah,* for the djellabah, or hooded cloak, they wore.

"Who are those men?" I once asked my father. He explained that they also lived in our country but were different from us; they had a different religion, were Muslim rather than Christian. According to my father, there were many of these kinds of people he called Juur—Arabs—in northern Sudan, whose border was several hours by horse from our village. Today, the Arabs did not come with their tea and sugar; they had brought guns and swords and were shooting Dinka men, slashing with their swords, chopping off heads with a single swipe. I had never seen such violence before, rifles that shot so many bullets at once. On our farm, to protect our livestock we kept old rifles that shot one bullet at a time.

And I had never heard so many screams.

"Run!" yelled Nyabol. "Leave your things and run!" I raced from the marketplace—and right into a huge horse with a militiaman pointing a gun at me. I stopped; I could not move. The thing that scared me most was a big horse, and here was the biggest horse I had ever seen standing in front of me like a wall topped by a man with a rifle screaming at me in a language I could not understand.

My heart was trying to leap from my body.

Someone grabbed me from behind. Another Arab, yelling at me and waving his gun. What was he saying? My mind was not working. I was sure he was going to kill me. All around me, I saw people screaming and falling on the ground and not getting up. But he pushed me back toward the marketplace with the other kids, boys and girls, those who could barely walk along with five-year-olds and bigger kids like me, ages seven to ten. Everyone was crying and screaming for their parents. I was crying, too. What was happening to us? The older kids, including my friends Kwol, Nyabol, and Abuk, were herded into another group and the women into a third. They were all crying. The Dinka men were lying all over the marketplace.

My parents were back at our farm. Scared, I wanted to be with the big kids from Gourion. They were supposed to be looking after me. But they were in the other group, and I was afraid to go to them. I looked around the marketplace for help, but all I could see were those bodies of the men, not moving, the blood running from them like water in little rivers going nowhere.

I had never seen a dead body before. When an old person in our village died they would not let the little kids see the body. Now I saw more dead bodies than I could count—some without heads, others looking as if they had just decided to lie down in the dust and go to sleep. How did I feel? People always ask me how I felt at that moment, and all I can answer is that I had never felt such terror, confusion, and helplessness before—or again. I wanted my mother; I wanted my father to pick me up onto his shoulders and carry me away from this. I felt so many feelings at once that I suddenly felt nothing. My entire body and mind turned numb as I waited to be killed.

But with no Dinka men standing, the killing seemed to be finished. While a few murahaliin guarded us, the others began collecting the food that was left in the market and loading donkeys with big baskets on the side. A man picked me up and deposited me in one of those donkey carriers. They did the same with the other little kids. Some of the women ran to their children, but the militiamen stopped them by beating them and pushing them way—and screaming those words that made no sense. They waved their guns, and the screaming, crying women turned quiet.

When the loading was completed, we headed out of Nyam-lell. Behind the horsemen, the soldiers, and our donkeys walked the older Dinka kids and women, forced to carry the very things that we all had been selling and buying not long before.

My mother had trusted me to go to the marketplace to sell her eggs and peanuts. The sun was going down in the sky. She would be expecting me to come home about now.

CHAPTER TWO

"ABEED"

We rode into darkness, my heart pounding faster than the donkey's hooves. My head was filled with questions: Why did those men do this? Where were they taking me? What about my parents? Would they be able to find me? Then I began worrying about them: Were they safe? The people in the market had talked about the smoke from the villages; they had pointed in the direction of Gourion, and talked about the burning houses. Was the storm of smoke coming from our houses with the straw roofs? The fear that something had happened to my family stuck in my throat.

But I was only seven years old and had little experience with worry. Quickly my mind replaced those concerns about my parents with the confidence that they would save me. I was sure someone would rescue me.

I was tired. Several hours had passed since the raid. But my mind would not let me sleep. In the middle of the night we passed through a forest and finally stopped in an open area. They took us kids from the donkeys and sat us down on the ground. Again, they yelled in their language. I said nothing.

I saw my friend, Kvol, and the girls, Abuk and Nyabol, but we spoke only with our eyes, which were full of fear. Everyone kept quiet—except two sisters, one about twelve, the other younger, who were crying. Through their tears they said they had seen their father shot and killed and their mother, too.

A militiaman grabbed the older girl, yelling at her, then trying to shake her into silence. She could not stop crying. He pulled her to the side, put his rifle to her head, and shot her. Right in the head, one shot that rang through the forest—*bang!* and when that noise finally stopped so had the girl's crying. He let her go, and she crumpled to the ground like an empty sack.

I wanted to fly away from this terrible thing, but I was stuck to the ground. My stomach was tightened by what my eyes saw.

Her little sister began crying even harder than before, her body twisted and pulsing with sobs. She had seen her mother and father killed, and now her big sister was shot dead before her eyes. She was crazy with crying, and our silence only made her crying seem louder. Suddenly, one of the murahaliin moved quickly to her side—and struck her leg hard with his sword, cutting it off at the thigh. We all stared at this terrible thing that no person should ever see: A big sword slicing off a little girl's leg, as if it were only the branch of a small tree. Blood squirting all over her.

I remember this, but I cannot remember if she stopped crying.

All I remember is the militiaman pointing to those girls, saying words that made no sense to me. But the message was clear: If you cried, you would be shot in the head or have your leg chopped off. I clenched my teeth to block my feelings from coming out. I was afraid my voice would scream out, and they would kill me. The other Dinkas stared at the little girls, who had done nothing but cry for their parents. A large fear sat on top of us with so much weight that we were unable to utter even a sound.

The murahaliin began dividing us between them. One of the men walked toward me and pushed me from the group. I pulled away to get back to my friends. He grabbed me hard. He was a strong man, not as big as my father, but over six feet, with curly hair and a gun slung over his shoulder. I started crying again. He pushed me toward his horse. I heard Abuk's voice:

"Piol! Where are you going, Piol!"

I looked back at her. She was trying to get to me but the men stopped her. "This is stupid!" she yelled at them in our language. "I have to take him home. His mother put me in charge!"

A man dragged her away, screaming and crying. All the kids were crying and screaming. "I want to go home!" I heard them yelling. "I want to be with my parents!" The women, too, were crying for their own children. "No, no please don't take her!" "Please, no. God help us, please, that's my boy, I want my boy!"

They were crying. I was crying. I, too, wanted my mother and father. But the man taking me to his horse said nothing. He just picked me up and sat me on a special seat to the rear of his saddle. I could not stop crying. Where was this man taking me?

I looked back at the others and saw Abuk, Kwol, Nyabol, and the other kids from the village going in different directions with different men. My body shivered with fear. I was scared of what was happening. I was scared of going with this man I did not know. I was scared of this horse. I had never been on a horse before. He pointed to a thing to hold onto and placed my hands on it. There was a leather belt that he wrapped around my waist. And then he swung his legs up onto the saddle.

When the horse started to move, I grabbed the horn, trying not to fall off. He spurred the horse into a trot, which bounced me all over the place, and I screamed for him to stop the horse and let me down. I was sure I would fall. He slowed the horse to a walk, looking back at me to make sure the belt was secure. I begged him to let me down, to let me go, to let me be with my friends, to let me go home to my parents. He said something that I didn't understand and then turned around.

We kept riding, the silence of the night broken only by my own sobs. I soon realized that my crying was not doing any good, and I stopped. A man I did not know was taking me someplace. Where? And what about my friends? Would I ever see them again?

I held onto the saddle, riding with this man, this Jur, who had attacked my people, whose friends slaughtered little girls, this stranger who shared our country.

We rode for another half hour and, as the sun came up, I noticed that the countryside was different. The trees were small, not like the big trees around our village. The houses were of mud and straw, but they were not shaped like the Dinka houses. I saw other people, but they were not like my people; they had lighter skin and wore the djellabah, and spoke the same language as the murahaliin.

I was sure we were now across the border in northern Sudan in the part where my father said the Dinka did not live, only the Arabs.

We rode through a village where the people seemed to know my militiaman. We kept riding, until we came to a farm. It was different from my father's place—not as beautiful. The house was like the other structures I had seen earlier, an Arab kind of house, one spacious enough for a whole family. He got off the horse, untied my belt, and, as he plucked me from my seat and set me on the ground like a package that he had brought home, some children came running out of the house—three of them, the oldest about twelve or thirteen, and then their mother, this man's wife. I was surprised to see a family. I had thought of him only as a murahaliin, an Arab on a horse with a gun who killed my people. It had not occurred to me that he might have a wife and children.

When I saw the children I suddenly felt better. They yelled to him, he said something to them. Happy to see their father, the children ran up and hugged him, just like my sisters and I embraced our parents. He embraced his wife. But she did not seem happy, at least when she looked at me. She said something to him; he said something back—and then something to the kids. I could tell from that woman's face that she didn't like me. But the kids ran up to me, laughing and talking. I had never seen an Arab child before, but noticed the younger boy was about my age. Maybe he would be my friend.

I wiped the sweat and tears and dirt from around my eyes. I wanted to show them what a good boy I was. I took a deep breath. The kids were laughing and yelling words I didn't understand. They seemed happy. Then they began singing, chanting the same word over and over, which sounded like *"abeed, abeed, abeed . . . abeed, abeed, abeed."* I was listening so hard, trying to understand this *abeed* song, I didn't notice they were carrying sticks—until they started beating me. The man's children, including the boy my age that I wanted to be my friend, chanted and laughed and struck me from all sides. I tried to block the blows, but the sticks stung my arms as if they had fire on them. Why were they beating me and calling me "abeed"? What did it mean? Something bad I was sure. But I was not bad. I had done nothing wrong.

"Stop!" I yelled, but they did not stop. I didn't think that I could experience anything worse than the slaughter in Nyamlell, my favorite place in the world running with the blood of Dinka men, and now these kids were laughing at me and beating me up, while singing a song, as if it were a game.

I turned to their parents. "Help me!" I yelled. "Why are these kids beating me?"

They said nothing, and the kids kept hitting me. "Help me!" I yelled. "Help me! Please, help me!"

But their parents did nothing but watch. My body buzzed from the blows. Marks were rising from my skin as if ants were building their houses on my arm.

The militiaman finally did stop them. But he was not angry with them; he was laughing, too. And as the kids and their mother went back into the house he made me get up from the ground and led me to an *evrik*, a small shelter made of mud and a flat straw roof located near enclosures for the goats and sheep.

He pointed to a blanket on the ground and left me alone. Big flies buzzed around my face. They landed on my arms and legs.

But I was too exhausted to care about the flies, more tired than I had ever felt in my life. I had not slept for one day, one night, and another day. I lay down on the ground wanting to sleep, still sobbing. But I could not fall asleep. My mind would not stop; it was going crazy with thoughts and feelings—so many different thoughts and feelings. All I could hear was the noise of the flies.

I could still remember how excited I felt when my mother told me that I could go to the market with the other kids. That was one of my dreams. I had realized that dream, and then within a few hours everything I had known for my entire life disappeared: my friends, my family, my village. And here I was with a different family, in a different world, in a situation I never could have imagined.

I rubbed the marks on my arm and legs, still burning from the blows from the sticks. But something else stung me even more. I realized that if the bearded man and his wife did not try to help me, then they didn't care about me. In my family, if I hit my sister my parents would stop me. When little kids fought in our village, their parents or other adults would break it up. I knew that you had to protect children from the cruelty of other children, because kids did not always know the difference between right and wrong. That was how my parents explained it to me. Never in my life had I been surrounded by people who did not care if someone was hurting me.

I had once seen a man whip his dog, and I felt bad for the poor animal. Maybe this was a crazy game these Arab kids played? Their father and his friends kill Dinka men in the marketplace, steal their children, and when they bring them home, the kids get to whip them like bad dogs. Would they beat me again?

Suddenly, there was a noise. It was the militiaman, and I stiffened. As he came closer, I saw that he was carrying a bowl, gesturing that I should eat what was in it. I just wiped the tears from my eyes and stared at him. He put down the bowl on the ground, pushed it toward me, and walked away.

I examined the contents of the bowl, which smelled terrible. It was some kind of hot food, unrecognizable to me. I had not eaten for almost two days, but I was not hungry. I was too sad to eat and pushed the bowl away. The flies rushed to the food, but didn't seem any more interested in it than I was. Sore and tired, I lay down on the blanket to sleep. But my mind would not let me sleep. I told myself that I must stay strong. My father would want me to be strong. It was hard, but I kept thinking about how I would see my family soon. But as I thought about them, I knew they would be worried about me. I was supposed to spend a few hours at the marketplace, and now I had been away from home for more than a day. They would have no idea who took me.

I looked around. No one was watching. I decided to run away from this place where children laughed at me, sang this word "abeed" and hit me with sticks. I stood up, but I did not know what to do next. Where would I go? Which direction? What would I do when darkness came? I could see the forest. Big animals out there in the black space could kill a little boy. My parents had warned me about tigers and lions that could run faster than a full-grown man, never mind a little Dinka boy who hadn't eaten for two days. I had no idea how to get back home. The only thing I knew was that I had ended up in the wrong place. But I could not leave now. I was too tired, too confused, too sad. Maybe tomorrow.

I sat down again on the ground. I looked around. The sight of this dirty place, near the animals, made me miss my family even more, and I began crying again. I cried until I had no more voice left to cry. My family would save me. That's what would happen. My father and my big brother Buk would come and save me from these Arab people.

I finally fell asleep.

CHAPTER THREE

THAT'S WHAT HAPPENS
WHEN YOU DISOBEY

The light of the sun woke me. At first, I was not sure where I was. But then I felt the pain in my body and heard the animals and realized I was still in this strange place, and my mind filled with everything that had happened in the past day and a half: the attack on Nyamlell, the gun pointed at me, the little girl shot in the head, her sister's leg slashed, my trip on the horse with the militiaman, the look of hatred on his wife's face, his children laughing at me and beating me as they sang their abeed song, sleeping in this shed like one of their animals.

My mind began thinking again of running away. But where should I run? It had taken so long to get here. I was just seven years old. How would a little boy like me find his way home?

My thoughts were interrupted by the arrival of the militiaman and his wife. The children followed. The family stared at me sitting on my blanket as if I were a new puppy. The kids started singing that abeed song again, pointing at me and laughing. The man handed me another bowl of food, some kind of meat, which smelled different to me from the food my mother gave me. The wife and the little kids went away, while the man and his oldest son went to the nearby enclosures, rounded up the goats, the sheep, the cattle, and camels, and led them to pasture.

They didn't seem to care that I was crying, that I was left alone in this strange place with my bowl of foul smelling meat with the flies buzzing around it. I shooed the flies away and tasted the food. Very bad. But I ate it anyway. I was too hungry to care how it tasted. I spent the rest of the day sitting in the evrik, thinking. In my mind was one question: When could I go home and see my parents again? It was the only thing I could think of. I wanted my mother to pull me close to her, to hug me.

For days I kept expecting that someone would arrive on this land, find me in the hut, and say, "This is a mistake. I will take you back to your parents." But no one came except the militiaman and his sons. His name, I soon figured out by listening to his wife talk to him, was "Giemma"—Giemma Abdullah. His oldest son was called Hamid, the other boy they called Jeju, and the girl was Haweh. I spent my days and nights in the evrik, afraid to move for fear that they would beat me again. Each morning the sunlight and the noisy animals would wake me, and soon Hamid would ride up on his horse and take the goats and sheep away for the day.

Hamid would say something to me, but I did not understand the words.

For the next two weeks I did not wander far from my blanket, a handful of dirt's throw from the family's goats and sheep. I could also see their horses and camels and cattle in a circular corral not far away. I could count only to ten, and counted many tens of cattle, many more than my father had, some that looked like the cattle we had in my village and others that were different. I had never seen so many animals in one place.

People said my father was ajak, a rich man. But this militiaman—this Giemma—was truly ajak. His djellabah was pure white, and he wore beautiful shoes, one day made of brown and white cow's skin, another of tiger skin. I had never seen such shoes. His wife's clothes were fresh and white too; everyone in this family was clean.

One morning I ventured closer to the house and saw Giemma's wife. She yelled at me and waved me away. After that morning, I did everything I could to avoid her. Whenever she saw me she turned her head away, as if she could not bear to look at me. I was afraid she would hurt me.

But there was another reason I kept my distance: Seeing this angry woman made me think of my beautiful, smiling mother, who gave me a bowl of cow's milk each morning before any of the other kids and told me what a good boy I was. My mother hugged me and loved me. When I thought of her, my mind raised images of the rest of my family and then my friends, and when I thought of my friends I remembered what fun it had been to go to the market with them. And then the shooting and screaming invaded my mind, and I also thought of that night when Giemma took me away and Abuk yelled, "I have to bring him to his family!"

I had stopped thinking that someone would arrive to rescue me. But I could not stop the questions: What would happen to me? Why was I with this family? Every day and every night I did nothing but think. I felt so alone, surrounded by people who only smiled when they beat me. I felt like the only Dinka boy left in the world.

One evening, when Hamid returned with the goats and sheep, Giemma came to me and pointed to the animals and then to his son and then back to me. His words still had no meaning for me, but what he was saying somehow was clear: Tomorrow I would go with Hamid and the animals.

The next morning Giemma and Hamid turned up as usual, nodded to me, and then let the animals out of their enclosure. As I watched, Giemma handed me a small whip, saying something I did not understand. But when they herded the animals out of the corral and toward the forest, I knew I had to follow. Two weeks before I had been a seven-year-old Dinka spending the day playing with my clay animals. Now I was working with real ones. I was scared of the animals, but I was more scared of getting beaten. If I refused to go, Giemma would turn his whip on me. That was clear.

What was still not clear to me was that this was my first day of slavery—being forced to work for no payment but the garbage from the family's dinner and an occasional beating from Giemma's big cattle whip.

We drove the goats toward the forest. Whenever one strayed from the herd, Giemma made me chase after it. This, I quickly learned, was my main job—to keep the crazy goats from running away, and most of the goats seemed crazy. It was not easy, running this way and that in the hot sun. Hamid and Giemma showed me how to use the whip to keep the animals in line. (The sheep were easy; they just trudged along, one

following the other). After a while Giemma sent us off on our
own. I was so busy running after goats, I didn't know that I
had passed my first test as a slave. Giemma headed back
home, while Hamid and I drove the animals toward the forest.

When we reached the edge of the bush I stopped. He signaled me to follow, but I was scared. My parents had taught
me that the forest was a dangerous place filled with lions and
tigers, snakes and insects that could hurt a little boy, even kill
him. And now it was my job to walk into that kind of danger.
Hamid yelled at me and waved me forward, and I obeyed. I
told myself that I would be safe in this forest with this Arab
boy who came here every day.

But I kept an eye out for trouble, looking around as I
walked deeper into the bush. As I looked, something among
the trees amazed me: another black boy. And then another!
They were probably twelve or thirteen years old, herding
cows. Were they Dinkas? I wanted to run to them, but Hamid
saw them, too, and he knew what I was thinking. He yelled
something at me and shook his head. I could not go near the
other boys.

It didn't matter. I was not alone after all. Giemma's neighbors were also rich with animals—goats, sheep, cows, camels,
and horses—and there were black boys taking care of them. I
was sure they were Dinkas. They looked like the kids from my
village. Maybe they spoke my language and could help me. It
was my first happy moment since going to the market. I felt as
if I could fly through the forest.

We reached a grassy area where the goats began to eat. A
few animals wandered away from the others, and Hamid and I
chased them back to the herd. Soon I seemed to be doing all

the chasing. After a few hours in that spot, Hamid began rounding up the goats and sheep, and I, with a snap of my whip, made sure the goats kept up with the rest as we drove them farther into the bush to another grassland. Hamid kept after me to chase the strays. But soon most of the animals had stopped eating and were lying around just chewing. Hamid signaled me to follow him as he rounded up the animals again, and we headed in another direction.

I was not sure what came next, until I heard a lot of noise up ahead and then saw the source: There were hundreds of animals drinking in a nearby river, and hundreds more—not just goats and sheep but cattle, camels, horses—waiting their turn. There were also more black boys, a few my age but most older, like the first two kids I had seen in the woods. I really wanted to talk to them, and Hamid noticed.

"No," he said, his gestures indicating that I must stay with the goats—and away from the Dinka boys. I obeyed. But at least I now knew that I was not the only Dinka in this world. An opportunity to talk to another Dinka would come, and I promised myself that I would seize it. I had so many questions to ask: Why had this happened to us? How long would we have to work for these people? When would we be able to go home?

Surely, these older boys would have some answers. But, when I did have a chance to get close to the other Dinka boys at the river, I was shocked to hear them speaking Arabic. Did they speak my language?

I answered at least one question that had been in my mind since I arrived: what did "abeed" mean? Hamid had referred to the other Dinka boys as "abeed"—the word that these north

Sudanese used for us black Sudanese. In fact, as I soon learned, for these Arabs *abd* (the singular of *abeed*, though pronounced the same) was a very useful word: it meant both "black person" and "slave."

Every morning I left with Hamid to continue my training as a goatherd. We made our way through the forest to a grassy place, and Hamid showed me what to do, using a combination of language and gestures. The job was easy to learn, even for a seven-year-old. First, the goats must eat—until they were thirsty. I would know that they were thirsty when they stopped eating and lay down. When all the goats were kneeling on the ground it was time to take them to the watering place.

That was the main challenge. The lines were long, and the goats—all the same brown and grey—could easily get mixed in with a neighbor's animals. The sun was hot, like sitting too close to a fire. Some days we had to wait for hours for our turn to let the animals drink. Once they had drunk their fill, I was instructed to take them back to the pasture. If that place had been eaten clean, then I would have to find a grassier place. My main responsibility, I soon began to understand, was to keep from losing goats. I spent a good part of my day chasing goats back into the herd. Hamid spent his days watching me at that task. Beyond telling me what to do, Hamid had little to say to a homesick Dinka boy almost half his age. Whatever conversation he offered, I could not understand. But I was beginning to make out certain words from the jumble of strange sounds. I listened harder, as if, by listening, this new language would become understandable.

Not long after I started working with him, Hamid showed up on a horse. As he rode into the bush like a half-sized mura- haliin, his djellabah flapping in the air, I followed on foot with my little whip, prodding the sheep forward and beating way- ward goats back into line. Later in the day, without a word to me, he climbed on his horse and rode away. For the next few hours I watched the sun go down, and worried about how I would get the animals back to their pens by myself. Hamid had always led the way. He was my boss, my young master. But he had abandoned me. I wished I had paid more attention to the way we had taken to the grassland. My fears about being attacked by big animals came back. I was lost and I was scared.

And then I heard Hamid's horse. He had returned. This, too, became part of our routine. Hamid's job was to spend his days with the animals (and with me), but occasionally he would ride away, probably to visit his friends. I never knew when he would leave or return. His freedom taught me that I had none.

I now had a bed. A wooden frame, nicely built, with palm leaves twisted into strips stretched across it for comfort. I was given one thin blanket to lay on top of the bed and another to put on top of me. This bed was a big improvement over sleep- ing on the hard ground.

But I hated my life. I hated taking care of Giemma's ani- mals, I hated the way they treated me; I even hated the food they made me eat—boiled meat without spices or sauce, some- times half rotten. I tried my best to hide my feelings, but did not always succeed. Some mornings I just didn't want to go with the animals. Giemma had an answer for my complaints, and the gestures that went with his words made it clear what he was saying.

"You don't want to get up and walk on your own two legs?" He pulled my legs from the blanket. "Then maybe you don't need two legs. I chop one off for you." He chopped his hand in the direction of my leg. "And then you can stay here and lie on the ground all you want."

I had been beaten many times, and I preferred working to being beaten, so I stifled my complaints and went to work. Whenever I showed any resistance, Giemma would use this same threat: "You want your legs cut off, okay, act that way."

He said this so often that I took his words only as a way to scare a little boy, a cruel threat, to be sure, but still only words—until one day when Giemma and I were returning from the grasslands, passing by a neighbor's property. I saw a Dinka sitting on a neighbor's property. I wondered why I had never seen this boy before, then saw the reason why and it shocked and sickened me: one of his legs was missing. There was a man in our village with one leg, who had lost the other, my father explained, "in a war." I had never seen a boy missing a limb.

"What happened to him?" I asked Giemma.

He looked over at the boy, then back at me, and smiled. "I told you that's what happens to bad boys. He tried to escape. They caught him and warned him. He tried again, and. . . ." Giemma shrugged as if to say there was no alternative for handling kids who didn't obey their master.

I stared at the boy with one leg, as Giemma kept talking: "These kids complain too much, they try to escape. That's what happens when you disobey. You want that to happen to you?"

I shook my head. But I was not answering Giemma's question so much as shaking off the horror of that missing leg. Escaping was my dream. It never occurred to me that I would escape, get caught, and have my leg cut off. When I ran away, no one was going to catch me.

CHAPTER FOUR

WHY DOES NO ONE LOVE ME?

"Abuya." Giemma kept saying this word to me. "Call me *abuya*." I did not understand. What was this word "abuya"? He explained that he was *ab* to Hamid and Jeju: Suddenly I understood: He was their father, and he wanted me to call him "my father"–abuya in Arabic.

I never called Giemma abuya. I already had a father–my *wawa*, the Dinka word for father–and he loved me. I often thought about my father. Was he looking for me? Did he miss me? I certainly missed him. By thinking of him, it was as if he were with me, sitting on my blanket, watching Giemma's goats. When my father was around I could not see anything else. He was seven feet tall, a huge and handsome man. He shined his love on me every day, something that became clearer to me now that I had to get through my days without hearing so much as one kind word.

I missed our daily talks. But some days he would tell me important things. "I know you're little, but you must listen to what I say." He would warn me that he would test me on what he said, so listen hard. I listened as hard as I could. "You will grow up to be like your father."

A few weeks later, he would say, "Do you remember what I told you last time?"

I said, yes, and told him exactly what he said: I would grow up to be like you.

"What does that mean?"

I had my answer ready: "It means that I will be rich like you, and people will come and beg milk from me. I will also have lots of cows, and lend them to people, and they will pay me back with more cows—just like you."

He smiled at me. "I want you to be a good man, a good member of the community. I want you to have a good life."

Giemma cared more about his goats than me. My father had always encouraged me, treated me as special. In southern Sudan, people often gathered together in the evening at about three. My parents would bring food to a neighbor's house, and the men would eat with the other men, the women with the women. Generally, the children stayed home. But sometimes my father would invite me.

"He can't go there," my mother would say. But my father insisted that I come along. He hoisted me onto his shoulders, and on the way he explained that when he was a little boy his own father used to bring him to meet his friends.

"I want to treat you like he treated me," he said. "I want you to be a strong person. That's why I spend so much time talking to you, teaching you, testing you by asking you to repeat what I've told you."

"This is my special son," he announced to his friends. "One day he will do important things."

With my father's words echoing in my head—"One day you will do important things"—I looked out at Giemma Abdullah's goats. I decided that this could not be my future. Giemma did not know that his little goat herder took after his father.

Like my father, I had dreams and ambitions. I wanted to be the important person he believed I could be. I promised myself that I would escape some day. I would come up with a plan. I was not yet sure exactly what that plan was, but I knew that, to fulfill my father's dream for me, I would have to get away from Giemma Adbullah.

Isolated from my father, all I could think about was the dreams he had for me. I was determined to achieve those dreams. Until then, though, I had to work with Giemma and his son.

The routine was the same for the first several weeks: Hamid and I taking the goats to pasture, learning how to get to the areas where the good grass was, and Hamid watching me run after the strays, off to the river for water, and then back to grazing until the sun began to go down in the sky, when we would head back to the enclosure where I would eat my dinner alone. I hated spending all my time with the goats. The days were long, and I dreaded the hot sun and the chaos at the watering hole. Most of all I hated not being able to do what I wanted. Just a few weeks before I was spending every day playing with my friends and following my father around his farm helping him work. "Go play with the other kids," he would say, but I would insist on helping him work. My brother tended our cattle, and my older sister looked after the goats and helped my mother prepare meals.

They worked. I now realized that what I did with my father was only playing at work. If I wanted to go off and fool around with my friends, I did. Now I had no choice. I could not even talk to the other Dinka boys, never mind play with them. I knew that if I refused to obey Giemma or his son they would beat me.

I was now a worker. I worked all day, every day. With no choice. My childhood was behind me. I was seven years old.

In my old life everything was fun. In this new place satisfactions were few. Even if I had something to laugh about, I had no one to laugh with. I took pleasure in the fact that Hamid did not seem to like tending the goats any more than I did. He seemed to act as if, if it weren't for me, he would be able to spend his days doing something that was a lot more fun. But if I had to be miserable, there was something comforting in knowing that Hamid, Giemma's oldest and favorite son, was also spending his days tending goats—in the company of a seven-year-old Dinka boy who could not speak his language.

This new world I lived in made no sense to me: The people were different, the smells were different, the food was different, the language was different. Quickly, I realized I could deal with the people, survive on the food, and supplement what I found disgusting with the berries and fruit I could pick in the forest. I could take those changes in my life.

But the one thing I could not take was being unable to understand what these people were saying. I was a little boy who had led a comfortable life; but now I didn't even have the comfort of comprehending what my masters were saying to me—or about me. I also wanted to be able to communicate my feelings to them. Surely, they would treat me better if they knew how lonely and hurt I felt. They did not seem to understand how badly they were treating me. No one in my village ever treated a little boy in this way. My mother hugged me. My father swung me up to his high shoulders like a sack of beans—and I laughed. Maybe if I could explain to them the differences between us, life would be better; maybe they would send me back to my village. Maybe . . . maybe . . . maybe . . .

I also decided that it was important for me to understand these people. They were rich and powerful. These *murahaliin* killed Dinka men and made Dinka women and children work for them. They were at the top and we were at the bottom. I had played enough games as a child to know the difference between winners and losers. My friends and I played with our spears, imitating Dinka warriors who could run through the bush carrying ten big spears. But the spears of seven-foot-tall Dinka fighters were no match for the machine guns of Giemma and his fellow *murahaliin*. No matter how fast you could run, they would ride you down with their horses or camels. What was it about them and their way of life that allowed them to dominate my people? The secrets of their power and wealth were in their heads, and I was convinced that the only way to sneak inside to steal those secrets was to learn their language.

But more than anything I wanted to talk to the Dinka boys herding animals through the forest and standing at the river, who spoke only Arabic to each other. I had to learn this language—which now seemed a wall of strange sounds that made no more sense to me than the bleating of the goats. I began to listen carefully to everything Giemma and his sons said to each other, and as they showed me how to do my chores. As the days and then weeks went by I began to distinguish certain sounds as words, realizing that those words were common, and some of them easily connected to Giemma and Hamid's gestures and my own work.

The only opportunities I had to speak Arabic were with Giemma and his son, and except for giving orders to me, they didn't talk much. Giemma was not about to waste his time in conversation with a seven-year-old Dinka. Whenever I tried to talk to him, to try out some words, he shouted at me and gave me a swat. And Hamid was riding off during the day to see his friends. There were only the goats to talk to—and myself. And when I talked to myself the conversation was in Dinka.

I grabbed my language lessons when I could, usually in the morning when Giemma or Hamid told me where we would take the animals that day. They kept saying this word *hanim*, and I quickly realized it must be the word for "goats." I pointed to my goats, said "*hanim*?" and Giemma nodded. It was my job to take the goats to places where they could eat grass and then to where they could drink water. *Sahl* meant "grass," and "water" was *maa*. *Haleeb* was milk. I began to pick up a working vocabulary in Arabic, word by word. I quickly learned, for example, that I said, *na'am* (yes), and they said, *la* (no). If I didn't hear a word over and over, I might forget it.

But Giemma and Hamid were full of the same orders, day after day, as they tried to train their seven-year-old goatherd: "Make sure you keep moving them to the new grass, the grass they like. Make sure they get their water, and then bring all of them back. Don't lose any animals."

Then again, when I returned, Giemma would count the goats and ask after their welfare: "Did they *hop* the grass at that place?"

I soon learned this important word that everyone kept repeating—*hop*. Giemma would ask, "Did the goats hop the grass there?" He would say, "That goat doesn't hop the small goat." "My son hop his horse." Hamid would say that he "did not hop working with camels." Hop, it became clear to me, meant "like" or "love," and with the knowledge of that word I was able to understand what Giemma liked and didn't like.

Clearly, he liked his animals. Their well-being seemed to be the subject of most of his conversations that I overheard—how they ate, how they drank, how they behaved. It was not always easy to find the right place for the goats to eat. There were certain grasses that they didn't like, and I had to learn that. Giemma wanted his goats to be happy, and it was my job to make sure they were. His animals were his wealth, and he cared about his wealth.

Soon, when I went to the river to water the animals and got closer to the other Dinka herders, my ear began picking up words in their conversations that I now understood—goat and water and grass, what the animals liked and didn't like, what the other boys liked. I practiced a few phrases on Hamid, and he nodded as if he understood. But he did not praise me for speaking his language.

Learning this new language was a slow process, but it was one of my few sources of pleasure. Not only did it divert my mind from my loneliness and misery, it gave me an occasional victory. I would understand something that the family said, and they would understand me. I was breaking through this wall of sound, word by word, sentence by sentence. It was hard work, and it seemed impossible that I would be able to understand these people, never mind talk to them in such a way that they would understand all the thoughts and questions that were piling up in my mind.

I had settled into my job as Hamid's assistant. We had two hundred or so sheep and goats to care for, but the responsibility was his.

One morning, as I waited for Hamid, Giemma showed up alone. He made it clear that I was on my own today. I would take the goats off to pasture without Hamid. I became very nervous and scared. What if I lost some goats? What if they ran away? I did not want to do the job alone. But I knew I could not refuse. He would hit me. If I lost goats, he would beat me; if I refused to go, he would beat me.

I herded the goats out of the enclosure and aimed them in the direction of the grasslands we had gone to the day before. A few wandered out of line, and I shooed them back to the herd. But all I could think about was that I had to feed the goats well or Giemma would beat me. If I lost any goats, Giemma would be even more furious. And then there were the dangers of the bush. I was certain some animal or snake would bite me. Suddenly I missed Hamid, with his horse and his gun and the ultimate responsibility for bringing all the goats back. The anxiety of this new burden flowed into my stomach.

I got the goats to the pasture without any problems. Having passed that first obstacle on my own, I remember thinking, "Maybe it will be good not to have Hamid always bossing me around. Maybe I would not feel so nervous all the time."

But before I could get used to the idea of working on my own, I discovered that I was not really on my own. I heard a noise—a horse—and there was Hamid at the edge of the bush, watching. He had come to check up on me.

And thus, as one fear vanished another took its place. After Hamid made sure I moved the animals to the next pasture and rode away, I soon began to worry about the river. Herds of goats and sheep from all around the area often showed up at the same time. Sheep looked the same. My goats were the same color and size of their goats, and I was afraid they would get mixed up. The biggest challenge of my first day would be not to lose animals at the watering place.

I worked extra hard to make sure none of my goats visited with another family's goats, and I managed to leave the watering hole with my animals. But throughout the entire day I never felt comfortable. I had this feeling that something bad would happen to me.

As the sun went down in the sky, I rounded up the animals and headed back. Giemma was there to meet me. I actually felt something that I had been missing for weeks—a sense of happiness. I was happy that I had made it through the day.

But my master was not smiling; he was looking at the goats.

"Some are missing," he said.

"No," I said. I could not believe it. I had tried so hard. As Giemma began counting them again, I looked at all the goats and sheep, realizing that I had never known exactly how many there were. It never occurred to me to count them. In fact, I could not count higher than ten. What had happened to those goats? Giemma finished his count—and hit me with hard with his whip. He yelled at me, and I just shook my head, as if I did not understand what he was saying. But I now knew enough Arabic to understand: "It is your job to make sure they all come back," he said. "Did you look in the grass?"

Ard sahla—the Arabic word for *grass*. Suddenly, I knew he was right. I had not looked in the deep grass. The goats ran in all directions, and the grass in places was so deep that there was no way I could see all of them all the time. Before Giemma could find Hamid to begin the search, a neighbor arrived leading the two missing goats.

Giemma's anger had the desired effect. I was so scared about losing another goat that every evening I counted the goats before I headed back. At first this was a problem because of my inability to count over ten. But I needed a solution, and I soon came up with one: I just watched the goats constantly, never permitting even one to stray too far from the others. Before I left for Giemma's place, I walked through the grasslands making sure no goat was hiding from me. But because I could not count them all, I was never sure that I had them all.

When I returned to the pen, Giemma would be waiting to count the goats. "Please, God," I would pray. "Let them all be there." Giemma would nod and say, "The goats are all here."

After about a week tending them on my own, I checked the goats before I left the pasture: all accounted for. But as I herded them toward the pen where Giemma would be waiting for me, my mouth went dry and my stomach churned with fear. Without even counting I realized a goat was missing, and I knew exactly which goat it was. The animal had been moving slowly all day, limping a bit. When we headed back I had noticed that he was still not walking well. What an idiot I had been not to keep a close eye on that one! He must have fallen behind the others and got lost. Giemma would beat me bad if he found out.

I tried to get the goats and sheep into the pen as quickly as possible before Giemma arrived, but I did not succeed. Giemma approached the pen, counting the goats as he walked toward me. I tried to act as if nothing was wrong, but Giemma quickly saw the fear in my eyes. (I would make it my job to get better at hiding my feelings and lying.) He made a quick count of the goats, and I waited for the explosion. I knew that I would be beaten, and there was nothing I could do about it.

And I was beaten. First he slapped me with his hand, and then he grabbed his whip and beat me some more. "You lose my goats and I will keep beating you!" he yelled.

We went looking for the goat, but didn't find him. I was sure I would be punished again. But Giemma just yelled at me, "Make sure you bring all the goats back!" The next day Hamid found the missing goat resting in the high grass. The animal seemed sick, and, sure enough, within the week the goat was dead.

I became obsessed with making sure I had all the goats every evening when I left the grasslands and before we arrived at Giemma's. I was scared about losing goats, scared of taking them into new areas. I learned where to go and how to get back. I trained myself to get better, more responsible. I got so good at my job that I never lost an animal again.

But the fear that something would go wrong that would earn me a beating never left me.

. . .

Looking back on that seven-year-old boy dealing with two hundred goats and sheep every day, I am amazed by his ingenuity—for the job and for coping with the fears. I was constantly balancing my fear of getting hurt on the job with the prospect of getting beaten when I returned with the animals. As I tried to minimize my on-the-job risks, I was increasing my odds of getting whipped.

Still, I began taking some risks. One of my main tasks was to find the best place for the animals to eat. No matter where I went, no matter how comfortable I was in that place, eventually there would not be enough grass for the animals, and that meant it was time to move deeper into the dangers of the bush to find better grass. I tried to sidestep that risk. When it came to the best grass for the goats or the safest place for the goatherd, I often chose to look out for myself instead of the animals.

It was, I now realize, my one periodic act of rebellion.

Hamid caught me cheating a few times. "You must do what we tell you!" he screamed, and would rush at me with a stick, beating me as much as he wanted to. And, even when I fooled Hamid, there was the problem of Giemma. He had a way of looking at the animals and knowing that they had not had enough to eat. When he found out that I had cut a corner, he beat me.

Driving the goats and sheep back home one evening, I decided that it was time to get some answers from Giemma. I had lived with him and his family for more than a month. I had so many questions piling up in my head, and now I believed I knew enough of his language to ask them.

I practiced what I would say. But when I saw Giemma I got nervous. I was afraid he wouldn't listen to me. "You have to talk to him," I told myself. "You must do it."

I walked straight up to Giemma, and, for the first time, I talked to my master in his language:

"Why does no one love me?" I asked him, using that word I had heard him and Hamid use so often—hop, hop, hop.

Giemma stared at me as if one of the goats suddenly had spoken to him. Or maybe I said it wrong and he didn't understand me. I tried another question that had stuck in my mind from that first day when Giemma showed me my dirty blanket in the evrik so close to where the animals lived:

"Why do you make me sleep with the animals?"

"Where did you learn that!" Giemma yelled, and hit me again and again. I said no more. Giemma stopped, stared at me, his face puffed up in anger, and then walked away.

I had asked my questions, and it made me feel good that I had been understood—even if the only answer I got was a beating. There was even some satisfaction in having annoyed Giemma. I didn't realize it at the time, but I now think that part of what was so nice about that moment was that it was an expression of my own power. Like cheating by bringing the goats to as few different pastures as possible in a given day, enraging Giemma was an act of rebellion—a small one to be sure, but no less satisfying.

The next morning as I prepared to take the animals to pasture I did not see Giemma. I did not see him when I returned that evening, nor was he around the next morning. But that evening, as I finished getting the animals into their pen, Giemma appeared and walked directly to me. I expected another beating. Instead, he looked at me and said, "You want to know why no one loves you and why you must sleep with the animals?"

Amazed that he had come to answer me, I could only nod my head at his question.

"I make you sleep with the animals," Giemma announced to me, *"because you ARE an animal."*

He let those words ring in my ears, words he now knew I understood: *Inta hiyawan*–because you are an animal. Satisfied with his answer and certain that he had put the little black slave in his place, he walked away.

For me it was a double shock. That Giemma felt he had to answer me was a surprise. That he waited two days was also strange. Had he worked on his answer for two days? But what really left me dazed, standing there at the animal pen, was that this man who had control over my life saw me as nothing different from the hundreds of bleating animals standing in their pens.

It certainly explained a lot about my situation: why he let his kids whip me with sticks as they would a stubborn donkey, why they fed me garbage from their table, why they left me to sleep and eat alone in an evrik that that was no better than animal pen.

Even for a seven-year-old boy without any schooling, the consequences of Giemma's pronouncement could not have been any clearer: I now knew that life would never get better for me with these people. I would have to find a way to leave.

That was the moment when I began planning my escape.

CHAPTER FIVE

ABDUL RAHMAN—THE
PERFECT SLAVE

Late in the day, with the goats well fed, well watered, and resting, I myself could rest in the shade of a tree and make plans to run away.

"Tomorrow I will leave," I promised myself.

Back at Giemma's, lying on my bed, when it was so black outside that the only thing I could see were the stars, I would change my mind. Where would I go? Even as a lonely, ignorant little boy, I knew I was too small and too weak to get far. I would have to hide in the forest where there were animals that would kill me. I was not only too little to escape; before I could run away, I had to learn many things.

I was learning the language. That would help me find help among these Arab people. But I also had to learn the area. I decided that each day I went out with the animals I would go a little farther in every direction. I would look around, investigate the roads, see who lived where, remember where there were men riding on horseback checking on their slaves. To escape I had to know that. And my primary goal in life was to get away from Giemma Abdullah and his family. I lived much of the day and night in my own head, and it was there in my thoughts—my memories of life with my family, and my dreams of escape—that I discovered freedom. Giemma and his family could beat me; they had total control of what I did every day. But they could not touch my thoughts and dreams. In my mind I was free, and it was there in that freedom that I planned my escape.

As certain as I was that I would one day escape, I also realized that that "one day" was far off in my future. Having passed so few rainy and dry seasons in my young life, my sense of time was limited. I judged the day by the rising and setting of the sun, and those days seemed endless. I had not been at Giemma's for even half a year, but it already seemed too long.

My misery and loneliness were compounded by what I missed about my previous life. Sometimes Giemma gave me milk in the morning. Giemma's milk sent me back to those mornings when my mother would present me with milk before any of the other kids. It was a rich cow's milk, much creamier than the watery version that Giemma gave me.

I missed my mother.

She was beautiful. I do not say that just because she was my mother. When I compare her to the other women in the village, she was the most beautiful. Her skin was lighter than mine, and she wore her hair a bit longer than the other women. Her body, too, was beautiful, and she moved gracefully, even when she carried a heavy load on her head. She was not tall, at least for a Dinka woman. I have seen women who were six-foot-six. My mother was only about five foot eight or nine. Her name was Adut Al (her father's name) Akok (her grandfather's name). Dinka women keep their family names.

Her family was wealthy with cows. It was big family with ten children—four boys, six girls. My mother was the youngest, and as the baby of the family she was always the favorite. My father knew her family well. They were part of the same Dinka clan my family belonged to. Her sisters were married to men my father knew, many of whom had the same name as mine, "Piol." A woman from a rich family like hers would have had a say in the man she would marry, and she chose my father. But as a successful man, he, too, would have had a choice. Families would have encouraged their daughters to marry a man with as many animals as my father. But he chose my mother, and, according to family legend, he had paid eighty cows—the ancient Dinka custom of "bridewealth"—to her family to get her.

Early in the morning when we woke up, she would give me milk first. "You like to work," she told me. "Whenever you follow your father and me around the farm, you always try to do something to help us. That's why I give you milk first, even when there is not enough to go around."

She smiled and handed me my milk. Every year, she made sure the family celebrated my birthday, also inviting my friends to join me for a special birthday glass of milk. I can still see her smile, and I will never forget the comfort it provided that first year with Giemma.

Giemma's wife never smiled at me. That woman never seemed happy, at least when I was around. I sensed that from the moment I saw her. In those first days she seemed to avoid me. A few times she yelled something at me, but I didn't understand the words. The look on her face, however, was perfectly clear in any language: She did not like this new Dinka boy.

It was only when I had learned some basic Arabic that

I realized how dangerous Giemma's wife was. Giemma had left the farm for the first time since I had arrived, maybe to go to the nearby market town of Mutari to buy or trade. I came face to face with her. She looked at me with that same look of hatred I had come to know; she pointed to me, and spat her words at me again. This time I understood what she was saying:

"I am going to kill you."

Every time I saw Giemma's wife, she would point at me and make a variation of that original threat. Sometimes she would just repeat, "I am going to kill you." Other times she would be more specific:

"If I had a gun, I would kill you."

Even Giemma later admitted that his wife hated me. He was not going to criticize his wife in front of me. He stated her hatred as a fact of life—of my life and his. But I knew that if he came to agree with his wife, she would kill me. Or he would do it for her.

Giemma needed me. His older son did not want to do slave's work. But that did not stop his wife from hating me. I did my best to avoid her, but sometimes I would run into her. "Don't look at me," she warned. "Don't even come close to me." I would say nothing. Another time she said, "I wish we had more goats instead of you."

Giemma brought me my food. When he was away she would send the kids with the food. And sometimes I would have to risk going to the house to ask for it. She treated me as if I were a diseased animal. If she couldn't kill me, she would stay away from me.

When Giemma left the farm, I did my best to keep out of that woman's way.

. . .

As I sat in the shade of the tree waiting for the sun to go down and wondering if I would ever feel happy again, I noticed some clay nearby and grabbed a handful. A goat made a noise. It was nothing. They continued to graze, and I continued to watch them. I soon realized that my hands were kneading and shaping the clay. It had been months since I had been taken north to live with Giemma, leaving my happy childhood behind me soaked in the blood of the marketplace of Nyamlell. And while few days would go by without me thinking of my family, I had already forgotten the games of my childhood. Not once had I thought about playing madallah, our stickball game, or alweth, the Dinka version of hide-and-seek. I had not even thought of my herd of miniature cattle. Were they still standing there in my cupboard in Gourion? Or had the *mura-haliin* stolen my cattle, too?

But my hands had not forgotten. They were moulding another small cow, as if they were not connected to this unhappy slave boy tending his master's goats. I followed my hands, trying to recapture the pleasure of it. I was living here on my own. No one seemed to care about me—unless I lost a goat. The pleasure I had known from the touch of my mother's hand, the delight I had felt when my father swung me onto his shoulders eight feet above the ground, none of those rewards was available to me as I cared for Giemma's animals. I had not had a happy day since my life had changed. But maybe I could make myself happy shaping a cow out of this piece of clay.

I patted the clay together in my hands, building and shaping my new cow's body. I began shaping his head—and then I stopped. I felt nothing but sadness. For, while my hands did their work, my head did its work, too, and suddenly all I could think about were the friends who used to make our toy cattle herds with me in the village. What had happened to my friend Kvol? Was he, too, sitting in a grassland not so far away, thinking about happier days? Were Abuk and Nyabol cooking for murahaliin?

Those thoughts of my friends were soon replaced by images of my parents—and their smiling faces were quickly pushed away by memories of Giemma and his family kicking me and hitting me and never allowing me to be with even one person I might be able to laugh with.

As much as I wanted to laugh, I could not make myself do it, because I was not happy. Even when something happened that I once would have found funny—a goat jumping up in the high grass and then disappearing, a goat again, no goat—I could not laugh.

But I could not cry anymore either. For the first few weeks I had cried every day, as if my crying would get something to change. But I soon realized that nothing would change. My crying did not bring anyone running to help me. I decided to cry no more. I would try to be normal. Even though Giemma's family might threaten me and hit me and feed me terrible food, even though they viewed me as another animal on their farm, I would try to be normal. I would do my job, follow their orders, stop crying.

I often dreamed of my family. In these dreams, I would wake up in the morning and my mother would be there. In other dreams I would see my entire family, and in some I felt the happiness of that day all us kids left the village for our journey to the market.

But I also dreamed of bad things, about that day when Nyabol yelled, "Run!" and I ran—right into a man pointing a gun at me and yelling something I did not understand. That nightmare kept coming back, because I now knew that he had yelled at me to stop, and if I hadn't he would have killed me.

I also had dreams where I would try to run away, but Giemma caught me and killed me, just as he often promised he would.

"If you try to escape, I will kill you," he said, over and over again.

And after all these dreams—the happy ones and the bad ones—I would wake up crying for the life I missed or the life I was living.

I decided to replace my crying with praying. "Please, God, help me." My ideas about religion and God were those of a seven-year-old Dinka boy. I reached out to my God, not because I knew that He was all-powerful or just or merciful. I knew nothing about those ideas. I was innocent of the Bible, the New Testament, and religious issues in general. What I knew about God was what my parents had told me, and, once again, what I had learned from my mother and father served me well.

"God is always with you," my parents had told me. "Even when you are alone, He is with you." Alone at night sitting in my hut, I remembered that. Driving the animals on my own through the dangerous bush, with one eye out for tigers and lions, I often assured myself, "God is with me." My father once said to me, "Even when you are one, you are two. If you are two, you are three." I liked how that sounded, and now I liked how it felt. And sitting under a tree in the grasslands, the only human in sight, I got some comfort knowing that God was looking out for me.

"When you ask God for what you need, He will help you," I remember my parents telling me.

I had never needed help as much as I did then, and so I prayed to God almost every day: "Please help me. I love my parents, and I want to have a future. I don't want to die."

I saw God as the protector of people like me–lost, away from those who loved me, and living among those who did not seem to care whether I lived or died. During those first few weeks under Giemma's control I was scared and lonely, and I cried. I now decided that when I was lonely or scared I would pray for God's help. When I moved through the forest I would say, "Please, God, keep the dangerous animals away." If I had to break up a fight between two animals, I would say, "Please, God, help me. Don't let the animals hurt me."

Thinking of God seemed to provide me with some comfort. I began to feel better. "God will help me escape," I told myself.

I would just have to wait a while to get bigger and stronger and smarter. Then God would help me get away.

"You must become Muslim," Giemma announced, and pro-ceeded to give me a new name–"Abdul Rahman."[1] I already

---

[1] Recently, I mentioned this to an American friend who knows Arabic. "Do you know what that name means in Arabic?" he asked me. I had no idea. "Servant of the compassionate one," he said.

dressed in the Muslim fashion, wearing the *araga*, the tunic-like, knee-length coveralls that the North Sudanese wear over their shirt and pants. Giemma had given me some cow-skin shoes, though far less beautiful than his own. He told me that I would have to pray with the family, and I would begin that day.

"Watch what we are doing, and do the same," he ordered. I watched them pray and tried to imitate their gestures. But I had no idea what they were saying.

"You will learn," he said.

To live with his family, Giemma said, I had to become a Muslim. If I did not pray with him, I was a *kafir*—an infidel. Muslims could not even touch an infidel, never mind eat with him. Infidels were unclean.

I didn't want to say those prayers. I also did not want to complain. I had seen what happened to the boys who complained. I said the prayers, but in my heart I was still a Christian.

Giemma began calling me Abdul Rahman. But my new Muslim status did not seem to affect my treatment. Giemma's wife still gave me bad food. She cooked it but never seasoned it the way she did for her family. To be able to work I had to eat. But no one cared what I ate. Often there was a piece of meat that was going bad. With so many animals, food was never scarce, and they had plenty of grain. But no one ever cooked me anything special. Occasionally, Giemma or Hamid would hand me the leftover beef from their evening meal, instead of throwing it in the garbage. But even when Giemma and I were off at a cattle camp, he would never hand me something from his plate, even though as a Muslim I was technically no longer "unclean." Giemma tried to use my new name, but more often he and Hamid called me *jedut*. "Dut" is a common name among the Dinka, and I thought that was why they chose it, as a kind of special nickname for their Dinka boy.

Then I discovered that "jedut" was the Arab word for those slimy, crawling things that I saw on a dead cow, those little worms. That's what their name for me was—"maggot."

CHAPTER SIX

BE CAREFUL

I counted every day, every month. In Sudan there are two seasons, the rainy one and the dry one. I arrived at Giemma's in the dry time, in April or May, when it is easy for the murahaliin to move into the south and raid the villages of the Dinka. The middle of the summer in Sudan, in July, is too hot to be in the midday sun. It is so hot that animals die—and people, too, if they work too hard and long in the sun. During the hottest times of the year my family rose very early, hours before the sun came up, to do much of their work in the fields and with the animals before the sun rose high in the sky. My mother would come back home in the late morning to begin cooking the big midday meal, and the men would soon follow, escaping the sun.

The days do not cool off until October and November. December and January are as cold as it gets in Sudan—50°F and often down into the 40s. I did not have different clothes for the different seasons. As it got colder, to keep warm I kept putting on more of the clothes I had: two old shirts Giemma had given me, then three, and then my *arraga* over all that.

Then the rains came, occasionally leaking through the roof of my hut. By February it is dry again, and the grass begins to get scarce.

"We are going," Giemma announced to me one day, explaining that the animals needed to eat, and the grasslands in our area had been eaten clean. This news surprised and confused me: Why would people so rich in animals need to move? But I soon realized that it was because they were so rich that they had to move. Their cattle, camels, horses, sheep, and goats never stopped eating grass, and in the winter grass was scarce in Giemma's part of Sudan, north of the Bahr al-Arab River in southern Kordofan.

Several times a year I helped the family pack up all their things and leave the farm near the village of Kerio to take the animals to a "cattle camp" where the grass was more plentiful. We packed everything onto wagons and camels, from clothes and cooking utensils to moveable houses, and drove days to the nearest winter grasslands where hundreds of other families converged, their camels and wagons equally full, their herds surrounding them.

Alongside these belongings trudged their slaves, black boys like me and Dinka girls. After we made camp, life continued as before for the next few months: I took my goats to the grasslands, watered them nearby, and when the sun went down I returned them to new corrals, exactly the same as the ones we had in Kerio.

As we waited our turn at the watering place in the cattle camp an Arab boy greeted Hamid. Standing next to Hamid's friend was a Dinka boy, about thirteen or fourteen years old. He smiled at me and said, "Salaam aleikom."

That surprised me. I still expected to hear the Dinka language from Dinka people, but he gave me the traditional Arab greeting, "Peace be with you." Those non-Dinka words silenced me. All I could manage was a nod. Hamid's friend walked away, and the Dinka boy followed.

A few days later he approached me again. This time he was on his own, and so was I. (Hamid must have been off talking to one of his friends.) He looked at me, carefully, deeply, as if he were trying to see my thoughts, and greeted me in Arabic again.

I gave the traditional answer: "Aleikom al-salaam" or "and upon you, too." He asked me if I was working for the Rizeigat or the Walletgi, two different groups of militia. Giemma was in the Walletgi, and I told him so. His master was with the Rizeigat, a more powerful group, and, I later learned, the most enthusiastic raiders of Dinka villages across the border.

"Are things okay for you?" he asked. My real answer would have taken a day to say, but I understood Arabic better than I could speak the language. I also realized we would not have much time to talk.

"I'm okay," I said in Dinka.

He seemed to be nervous and kept looking around to make sure no one was listening. And then, in the Dinka language, he asked me where I was from. It was a slightly different dialect than the one we spoke, but I was still happy to hear my own language and to be able to speak it.

"Aweil," I said, which was the name of the biggest town in my part of Sudan, and a geographical distinction also used by the people to describe the area for miles around the town, a kind of county. He smiled. He, too, was from the Aweil area, a village called Muchara Dut, which was not that far away from my own. His name, he said, was Bejuk.

"Are there other boys living with you?" Bejuk asked.

I told him I was alone.

"Be careful," he warned.

I told him I hated working for these people.

"Don't complain," he advised. "You are too young. But you should know this is a very dangerous place. Do your job."

He told me that when kids complained or got lazy, they "got hurt."

I told him that my master and his kids had already beaten me. He shook his head, as if that were the least of it.

"They will really hurt you," he said, and then—as if it were difficult for him to say what came next—he paused before he whispered: "They cut a kid's leg off." He told me that a lot of kids had been hurt and even shot trying to escape. He looked around again and then back at me, and returned to speaking in Arabic.

"Don't ever talk to me in Dinka," he warned. "Not even a 'hello'. It will get me in trouble. You, too. They will beat us if we talk Dinka. They think we're planning to do something wrong, to escape."

I assured him I would talk only in their language.

"I must go and do my work," he said. "You go and do your work."

I nodded.

"Be careful," he repeated.

He left me alone with my thoughts, which included the image of the boy I had already seen with the missing leg.

Bejuk's words echoed in my head: "They cut a kid's leg off—for escaping."

A few weeks later, in February, I turned eight years old.

The days, the months, the rainy seasons, and the dry seasons went by, and I was now counting the years. Even as a little boy back in Dinkaland with my family, I had come to know the idea of a year and its passing from the family celebrations of our birthdays. Farm boys like me learned quickly the rhythms of a passing year by the seasons—that beans got planted during one part of the year, the rains came, the fields got green, and then the beans got picked. After the coldest months of December and January, I knew that the warmer sun was announcing my upcoming birthday at the end of February. And, while we did not have a clock and no one wore a watch, I did not have to go to school to learn that nature had its own clockwork for when the cows and goats had their babies. Giemma, too, as a farmer and herder, lived according to the requirements of his land and animals. As Muslims, every year, Giemma's family—and their slave—fasted from sunrise to sunset during the holy month of Ramadan. And as I became more fluent in Arabic, I would hear Giemma talk with his sons and friends about how the past year had gone and what blessings Allah might bring in the new year. I did my job, tried not to complain, and there were few problems between me and the family. As I got older the beatings got rarer, though Giemma's whip was always within his reach. Five years had passed; I had settled into their routine with my sheep and goats. When it was time for the family to move, I helped them pack and did my job wherever we went. When the animals were fat and happy, I helped the family pack up for the trip back to Kerio. More often, Giemma, Hamid, and I would leave with the animals for brief stretches of time—a few weeks, a month—in search of better grass. Sometimes, after a severe series of long dry seasons, we would travel as far south as the Bahr al-Arab River, joining large groups of Arab herders also in need of water. My biggest challenge still was not losing animals at busy watering places. I never lost my fear of the dangers of the forest, though I had yet to see a lion or tiger. But there were plenty of big snakes to be avoided, and one day we found three missing goats who looked like they had made a tasty meal for a lion.

I seemed to be succeeding at my job. I did not remember the last time I had been beaten. I was now thirteen years old.

"You take good care of my animals," Giemma told me, and those words gave me a day of happiness. But most days I was sad, hating my work and this family who kept me so isolated from them and the other Dinkas. I thought often of my parents.

But I was well aware of how much worse things could be for me, and I believed that God was looking after me, just as my parents had promised.

They probably would not have recognized me now, for when I looked into the water where I took my goats, an older boy looked back. I was now almost as big as Giemma and already taller than Hamid. I told myself that my parents would be proud of me. I was a good worker; more important, I was smart enough to stay out of trouble and win my master's trust. As much as I disliked my work, taking care of the goats and sheep was now easy for me. I was also working on my own, though I knew that periodically I was bound to see Hamid on his horse, checking up on me. The area was full of other horsemen, making sure their own cattle were being cared for by their own Dinka boys.

Then Giemma complicated my life again.

"Tomorrow, you will begin working with the cows," he announced.

Again, that feeling in my stomach returned. I protested that they were too big for me to handle, too dangerous. But Giemma disagreed. I was now big enough to move up from goatherd to cattleman. Giemma did not understand that it was not only the size of the cows I found dangerous as well as their sharp horns. In Sudan cattle are a measure of a man's wealth, and one cow was worth two goats—and more than any one abeed. It was as if Giemma had handed me a box full of jewels for safekeeping. I did not need this responsibility. To me, taking care of Giemma's cattle was only one more way of getting myself into trouble—and making it harder for me to get away and find my family.

Giemma, however, had made his decision, and the next morning I went out with him, driving six hundred head of cattle to pasture. The job was not much different from handling the goats and sheep: plenty of good grass, hours at the watering hole, more grazing, resting, and back to the corral.

But the size of my new animals mattered. If a goat got out of line, you just had to give it a smack with your whip. If two goats got in a fight, you could tear them apart. But when two bulls went at it, all you could do was get out of the way. The males often fought, slamming into each other, trying to gore the other to death with their sharp horns. I had watched one cow try to kill another, and I did not want to be on the other end of those horns, which could tear a grown man apart, never mind a thirteen-year-old boy.

To Giemma, my job was to take care of his animals—first the goats and sheep, now the cattle. To me, my job was to do what Giemma wanted—and keep from getting hurt. Dealing with the cows, the odds of injury increased. Giemma gave me a whip to prod the cattle on their way; but even so, I knew that a skinny thirteen year old was no match for a thousand pounds of beef.

What would happen to me if I broke an arm or a leg? My cows did not care about my safety, and I had no reason to believe that Giemma would take care of me if I got hurt. I had to keep myself in one piece. My dreams of leaving this family one day and finding my own people depended on that.

No sooner did I manage to master dealing with Giemma's large herd of cattle than he announced that he would be adding more than one hundred camels to my duties. I was so angry that I blurted out what I really thought—and should never have said.

"I don't want to take the cows and camels together!" I protested, explaining the camels were not only two big for me to manage, they were also too slow and lazy. In the middle of our trek to the grasslands, a camel could decide to lie down and go to sleep. Meantime, the cattle could trudge forward, forcing me to run back to try to coax the camel up and then rush after the cattle to make sure they were okay. "I will only take the cows," I told Giemma. "That's my job, the cows."

"Shut up!" Giemma yelled. He was furious. My job was to do what he told me.

"Let me give you some advice, Dut. You do not want to work, I can shoot you. Or maybe I just cut off your legs and you can stay home."

I took the camels with the cows, and I never complained again—even on those days when all the goats and sheep were added to my herd because Hamid was not available to take care of them. While it may not seem like such a hard life for a Dinka boy to tend an Arab family's herds—by age eleven or so I would have been watching my own father's animals—there was an important difference: If I made one big mistake working for Giemma, I knew something terrible might happen to me. Whenever I forgot how bad things could get for me, I would see another Dinka boy about my age missing a leg or an arm.

My plan was to do the work and be as cooperative as I could be. Giemma liked me for that, and often told me, "You take good care of my animals."

But he did not know what was in my heart. For inside me there was the hope that some day I would get away. I wanted to build on Giemma's trust, to get as much independence as I could, and then, one day, when I was far away from the family, with the cattle, I would run away.

I always knew I would escape. That dream was the only thing that made my heart smile. Some days I would treat my loneliness by thinking of a reunion with my family. That thought alone could make me laugh out loud and lighten my day. And even during those moments when I doubted that I would ever see my family again, I was still confident that

I would get away from Giemma and his family. That thought, too, put a smile on my face.

Giemma thought I was a good little dut, a dumb little worm who never complained. He had no idea that every minute that I was working for him, doing my master's work, I was thinking of that day when he would come looking for me in the morning and I would be gone.

I had already decided that my escape should come soon. Maybe in a couple of months, in the dry season, when I was older—when I was fourteen.

CHAPTER SEVEN

THIS IS YOUR LAST
NIGHT ON EARTH!

The days were always the same: in the morning take the cows to eat, stand in line for hours in the blazing sun to get water, back to the grassland, and then home as the sun went down. When the day was over, I would say to the cattle, "*Yalla al-beit*–it's time to go home."

But my real home was hours away to the south, where my parents and the Dinka people lived, and one day during the dry season, as I was herding the cattle to the grasslands, I decided that it was time to make my move. I was now as tall as Giemma and bigger than Hamid; walking in the forest did not scare me as much as when I was a little boy. As I tended the cows, I had also explored the area around Kerio. I knew there were roads not far from the grasslands where I had been going for years.

This was my seventh summer with this family, and I had learned a lot. They still hated me and fed me bad meat and scraps from their table. Giemma and his kids barely spoke to me, and my master kept me away from the only other people in the area who would have wanted to talk, the other Dinka boys. Even when I tried to talk to Giemma, he would wave a hand at me and say, "Shut up!" My social life was limited to grabbing a few quick sentences with another slave at the water hole. In Arabic. I was fluent now in my master's language. I even knew prayers from the Koran that I was forced to say with the family.

I understood so much. Above all, I understood that even if I stayed in Kerio seven more years, my life would not get better. Giemma would never say, "I will release you so that you can be free to do what you choose." He would never even say, "You are tired today. You don't have to go out with the cattle. Just rest."

I knew that I would never hear a kind word from these Arab people. Forcing me to do their work was to their advantage, and they did not care about a Dinka boy's comforts or interests. Although the concept of slavery was not clear to me, I understood that I had been taken from my family against my will, that I was working for Giemma against my will, that I could not visit the other Dinka kids against my will, and that Giemma and his family could beat me against my will. And when I saw the other Dinka boys working as hard as I was, not speaking Dinka for fear they would have an arm or leg chopped off, I knew that Giemma and his neighbors were using us. They attacked my people, killed the men, took away the women and children. I had seen this. I had seen men shot to death in the marketplace. I had seen a little girl shot in the head and her sister's leg chopped off. I was here, living with people I hated and who hated me.

Something was wrong. And while I did not know I was a slave, I certainly knew I was not free. My body hated the work

and the beatings; my mind hated the isolation. My only pleasure was to think of the comfortable days I had spent with my
family, longing to experience that kind of happiness again.
After seven years on Giemma Abdullah's farm nothing had
changed, and I knew the future would be only more of the
same—with the possibility of much worse if I made a big mistake. The only way to improve my life was to leave. I had been
thinking about my escape for years now, but that day I decided
that it was time to act.

"Tomorrow," I announced to myself. "I am going to do it."

That night I was so excited that I could not sleep. All I
could think was, "I'm going to leave them. They don't know.
Early in the morning I will head out with the cows as usual,
but I will not return." But I was also nervous, very scared. If
they caught me, I knew that the worst could happen.

Before the sun came up I took the cows far into the forest.
At this time of the morning only other slaves would be up and
about. I figured I was less likely to run into one of Giemma's
friends or neighbors. I was excited and scared about what
came next. The cattle began grazing, and I left them there.
I ran as fast as I could toward a nearby road, a big road that I
knew took people to different towns and villages. When I
reached the road I kept running. But soon the road forked.
Which one to take? It didn't matter. All roads went somewhere, and that somewhere was bound to be better than life
with Giemma's family. I chose the left fork, the one near the
trees. I could always slip into the trees to hide.

I ran for about twenty minutes, still a little scared, but filled
with a sense of mission. After seven years I had finally done
what I had dreamed of doing. Most important: I had made

a choice, my own choice. As frightening as it was, the exhilaration of my freedom powered me down the road away from Giemma's farm.

Suddenly, up ahead, I saw some cows—and then a man on a horse. My stomach swirled: If he saw me, it was over. I quickly turned around and began moving quickly in the opposite direction, hoping to make it into the forest. Within seconds, I heard the horse at my back and then in my way. My escape had failed. But what would come next?

"Where are you going?" he asked.

My mind was racing. I gestured to the forest and told him that a cow had run away and I was looking for it. He looked around, and I knew what the next question would be:

"Where did you leave the rest of the herd?"

"Close," I said, adding one more lie to the first. He then asked me what group I was working with, and I told him the truth: the Walletgi. The rider said he was with the Rizeigat.

"Who do you work for?"

"Giemma Abdullah," I said. He nodded. Giemma's family was well known in the area. His older brother, Moussa, was high up in the Walletgi militia, and this man, whom I later discovered had a farm not far from Giemma's, knew who they were.

"Let's go back," he said. I said nothing. He left his cows there and rode alongside me.

"You're not chasing after a cow; you're trying to escape," he said.

I said nothing.

"Do not try to escape," he advised me. "Giemma will hurt you."

He may have kept talking to me. I don't remember. At the time, my mind was far away. I was definitely scared about how Giemma would react to the news of my attempted escape. But when I think back to that moment, what dominated my mind was the thought, "It didn't happen this time. But I will make it happen."

When we got back to Giemma's, he was dressing up to go someplace. He saw me and a look of surprise crossed his face.

"Why are you back so early?" he asked me. Then he saw the man on the horse. They talked, and the man explained that he had seen me running down the road, that I had made an about-face when I saw him, and that I had given him a story about chasing after a runaway.

Giemma looked at me. "Did you do this?"

"No," I said.

He looked at the other man, who simply said, "Yes."

Giemma asked me how far away the cows were from where the man found me, and I told him that they were right nearby. The man told Giemma that the only cows there were his own, and that's why he knew that this abd was trying to escape.

Giemma grabbed a cattle whip and started beating me. I did not protest. In fact, I was relieved that he was not going to chop off my arm or kill me for trying to escape. When he stopped hitting, he warned me, "If you try this again, you're gonna be like those kids we saw. I will hurt you."

I kept quiet. I had nothing to say to this man who was beating me with a whip. I still had my dream. I knew what I wanted. Giemma had control of me now, but my mind was free. To prove it, I chose to say nothing.

Giemma and the Rizeigat went looking for the cows.

. . .

The next morning Giemma took the herd to the grasslands himself. The following morning, I told Giemma I would take them. He stared at me.

"Do not try to escape," he warned.

I assured him that I would not do that again.

"Don't leave these cows alone again," he said. "Do not even try to take them to the same place all the time. Keep taking them to different places. The best grass."

"Yes, Master."

I headed off to the grasslands with the cows—and my plan to try to escape again. Today I would spend the day in my usual routine, in case Giemma had sent someone to spy on me. But when the sun began to go down, instead of herding the cows back to Giemma's, I headed for the road again. This time I went in the other direction.

But I stayed in the woods, following the road which I could still see as I ran through the trees as fast as I could. About an hour later, I reached a turn in the road and saw a little river nearby where some people were washing up for evening prayers. There were also some slaves hanging around. Tired and thirsty, I decided I could risk a short rest before moving on. Everyone would assume I was working. I walked to the river's edge, knelt down, and then looked around. No one seemed to be paying any attention to me. I scooped some water to my face. It felt cool. "I am on my way," I said to myself.

I scooped another handful of water and washed the dust and sweat off my arm. But it did not feel so good. Another feeling had taken over, one of danger. It was as if trouble had stepped up behind me and was looking over my shoulder. Something was wrong. I turned around and my trouble was only a few yards away. He was tying his horse to the cart. Giemma! Was my mind fooling me? My master had appeared out of nowhere, as if in a bad dream, to catch me in the act of escaping.

But it was no dream. It was Giemma, all right, who had probably just given his horse a drink in this same water I was using to wash up, and the sight of him where he was not supposed to be was like a punch in the stomach. He saw me. His next step was toward me.

"What are you doing here?"

"I'm just getting water, a drink. The cows are here."

"Where?" Giemma looked around, seeing no evidence of his cows.

"Not far," I said, lying again, yet knowing that I was only delaying the inevitable. The cows were miles away, on their own.

"Let's go get the cows," said Giemma, and he headed back to his horse and wagon. So, with Giemma leading his horse, we went looking for the cattle. I think at first Giemma actually believed me. He did not think I would be crazy enough to try to escape two days after I had been caught and beaten.

We kept walking, and there were no cows.

"Maybe they moved," I said.

"But you said you just stopped for a drink," he noted. "How could they go too far for us to find them?"

I had run out of lies. And I could not make cows that were not there suddenly appear. But I knew it didn't matter. Giemma was now very upset.

"You tried to escape again."

I said nothing.

"I can tell," he said. I waited for his hand to hit me, but all he said was, "Let's go home." He signaled me to get into the wagon, and I did. We drove back to his house, in silence. I was frightened by what awaited me at the end of this ride. Images of Dinka boys with arms and legs missing filled my head. He had warned me the other day that if I tried again, he would hurt me. As the cart jiggled along the dusty road, I was hoping that Giemma would kill me instead of cutting off my leg.

When we arrived back at his place, Giemma stopped the horse, grabbed my hand, and led me into the house. His family was there. Giemma explained that I had escaped again. He had stopped for water and accidentally confronted me. Giemma cursed me and smacked me several times with his hand. I said nothing. I don't remember how much he hit me; I felt nothing but anger at myself for failing to escape.

"Kill him!" his wife yelled. "Don't beat him, just shoot him. I don't want him. I don't want this abd around."

Giemma grabbed a thick piece of rawhide and led me to a room, pushed me to the floor, hitting me a few more times.

"Tonight will be your last!" he shouted. "You did not listen to me." As his wife and three children watched, Giemma tied my hands behind me and then my legs. He tied me so tight that it hurt. Then he told Hamid to go with him to get the cows.

I sat there in the room, filled with anger against my own stupidity. Soon, however, my hands and feet began to hurt. But no matter how hard I tried to loosen the rawhide, it seemed only to get tighter.

The time moved slowly; my body was uncomfortable—tired, hungry, and thirsty. My mind was filled with ideas of what Giemma would do to me when he returned.

Giemma slammed through the door, and his wife was behind him, remaining outside. He was carrying his cattle whip and his gun. He pointed the gun at me, and then said simply, "This is your last night. I will kill you tomorrow."

Giemma dropped the whip and slowly aimed his gun at me. "Shoot him!" his wife yelled. My only thought was, "Would it hurt?" He kept the gun on me, and I waited for the bullet. "Whatever happens now, happens," I said to myself. I did not look at Giemma or his rifle.

Then Giemma surprised me again. "I will kill you tomorrow," he said. I looked at him as he lowered the rifle.

"I don't want him!" his wife protested. He left the room, closing the door.

I cried with relief, and then I cried over the fact that this would be my last night on earth. A little while later, Giemma came back into the room.

"I told you if you tried to escape again I would kill you. I'm going to do it." I didn't look at him. He left the room again.

It was uncomfortable sitting on the floor. I slid myself to the wall so I could lean against it, then tried to get my hands and legs free. But the more I stretched and strained at the rawhide, the tighter it seemed to get, rubbing my skin until my wrists and ankles were bleeding. I cried in pain, but more in frustration for my failure to get away.

A few hours later, he returned with some water and food.

Noticing I was bleeding, he loosened the rawhide slightly and left. I was alone again with my thoughts. I was not hungry.

Giemma returned one more time. "You lied to me," he said. "You said you were with the cattle." He did not seem to expect an answer, and I gave none. It was as if he wanted to give me an explanation for why he was hurting me. Giemma seemed to want to justify his behavior to me, his slave.

"I knew you were lying when you said you were just getting a drink and the cows were close," he said. "It was the same thing you said the other day."

He stared at me, but I said nothing. Then he shook his head. "You think you're so smart. But I am smarter than you."

He left me alone with my sore body and mind. It was the middle of the night, and I was tired and in pain. The skin on my arms and back was red and swollen from where he hit me. His whip had torn my shirt. My wrists and ankles ached under the rawhide. Giemma knew I was tired and miserable, and perhaps his periodic appearances that night were part of the torture. Maybe he expected me to beg for forgiveness, to plead for my life.

I said nothing to him. But I had no doubt that in the morning he would shoot me. I had tried to escape twice in two days, and he had promised me—and his wife—that he would kill me. I decided that being shot would be better than having my leg chopped off. I would be dead and finally through with this place and this family.

My mind preferred death. But for some reason that I did not understand, I wanted to live. My mind told me death would be better than this life, but I—Piol, Francis Piol Bol Buk—did not want to die. I began praying for God's help.

"Please, God. Don't let him kill me."

Sitting alone in that room, my hands and legs bound, my body aching, my mind filled with thoughts of death, I prayed to the only one that could help me now. God had helped me before. He was all I had now on my side; I didn't want Him to abandon me now. God was my only way out of this.

"Please, God, give me some good ideas so that I can see my parents again. I love them, and I want to live for them."

CHAPTER EIGHT

THE DOUBLE GAME

I don't remember sleeping at all that night. I remember only my anger at myself for having failed, the fear of being shot, and the prayers that made one night seem longer than the seven years I had spent with Giemma's family.

A while later—it was still dark outside—Giemma returned. I stiffened. This was it. He stared at me, and what a pathetic sight I must have been, tear-stained, the blood caked around my wrists and ankles. I looked at him and noticed that he did not have his gun. He didn't even have his whip. He walked over to me, bent down, and began untying me. Then he looked into my eyes and said, without emotion, "If you do it again, I will kill you. I promise."

All the feelings of the night rose in me—the anger, the pain, the fear—and I was happy. God had answered my prayers. Giemma was not going to shoot me today. As he finished untying me, I said, "I will not do it again."

"I do not want to kill you," Giemma said. "You take good care of my cows."

. . .

Over the next few days, I sat on my blanket in the evrik hoping that Giemma would not change his mind. I was scared, and I am sure Giemma could sense my fear. I was no longer thinking of escaping. I only had to look at the marks on my wrists and ankles, still swollen and caked with dried blood, to remind myself of how close I had come to dying. So much fear had filled me that night that it was still inside me.

Giemma would show up, and my heart would race.

"You will not try again?"

"No," I promised. He left me alone.

And then the next day, he returned. "You're not thinking of escaping again? You're going to do your job."

"Yes, master."

"I don't want to kill you."

I said nothing.

"You take good care of my cows."

"I will."

"No more escaping."

"No more."

Giemma stared at me, and my eyes reflected my fear. I had lied to Giemma many times before, but not that day. I was telling him the truth: I was not thinking about escaping. To do so was to be reminded how close I had come to dying.

Three days after my escape attempt, Giemma told me to go back to work. I promised that I would never do such a crazy thing again. I would always stay with his family, and to prove it I kept doing my job. My biggest ally was Giemma. I might be just one more abd to him; he might consider me "an animal." But I knew that Giemma liked his animals, and I would make sure I was the hardest working animal on the property. My job became my lifeline.

That fear of dying stayed with me for days.

But fear, I had discovered, was just like pain—it, too, disappeared. You jammed your toe against a rock, and it hurt, but the pain soon went away. They beat you, and you begged God for the beating to stop, and it did. Your arms and legs buzzed with pain, but a week later you had forgotten that the beating ever happened. The night that I sat in Giemma's house waiting for him to come and kill me, I was filled with fear and could think of nothing else. But a few days later I was watching my cattle drink at the watering place, as if I had never been scared in my life.

So I did not lie to Giemma when I told him I would never escape again. But I soon realized that, while the pain and fear came and went, the one thing that never seemed to go away was the ache of wanting to escape this place where I was forced to work and live like an animal. I did not always think of escaping; I did not always want to think of escaping. But whenever I had nothing else to think about, my mind snapped back to dreams of returning to my family.

I was confused. I did not want to die, but wasn't living with these people a kind of death? Sometimes I wished I was dead, that I had been cut down in that marketplace in Nyamlell. But then I would see Giemma's wife and she would threaten to kill me, and suddenly I did not want to die anymore.

What did I have to live for?

The answer was always the same: my parents. They would be so happy to find out that I was still alive. I would walk into Gourion almost a grown man. My parents would see me, run to me, and hug me, just like they did when I was a little boy.

. . .

I began thinking about escaping again. My new plan was to
wait another three years before I tried again. I am not sure
why I picked this number. But I would have to regain
Giemma's trust. I would have to prove to him that I was not
thinking of escaping. I think I also realized that in three years
I would be about the same age my older brother had been
when I was kidnapped. He was already a man. At seventeen I
would be a man, like my brother and father. I would be
stronger, smarter, and better prepared to get away.

So I focused on my work. I tried to do the best job I could,
and as the months passed, Giemma seemed happy with me.
And at every opportunity he encouraged me by reminding me
of the alternative. "If you try to escape again," he said, "I'm not
going to beat you, I'm not going to cut off your legs, I'm just
going to shoot you."

I believed him. But Giemma needed me. If I were not doing
the work, he would have to help Hamid tend the animals. With
me helping, Giemma was able to work on his house. With me
spending the day with his cows, he was able to go to the market,
to trade, and to buy more animals. With me working for his family, he was able to go off on his annual raids to the south to kill
more of my people and steal their cattle. Because of me, he and
his family were able to move during the dry season to the grasslands. Giemma was a wealthy cattle owner, and I was raising his
cattle. Without me taking such good care of them, more would
have died. Giemma knew that, and I knew he needed me.

I had to continue to be indispensable to Giemma. This man
had his farm to run and his family to care for. He risked his life
on those raids in the south. I understood that Giemma had his

own problems, and if I became just one more problem for Giemma he might take his wife's advice, and I would never see my parents again.

For the next three years I did my work better than any boy in the area. I did my job so well that Giemma even praised me to his wife.

"Why are you keeping him?" she would ask. "Why don't you kill him? I don't want him."

And Giemma would always say, "He takes care of the cows. He does a good job."

When I think of this, I am amazed at how much Giemma trusted me. He had no idea what was going on in my mind. I guess he did not think I had any mind at all. He treated me as an animal, and animals do not think. I had now spent half my life among Muslim people, and I understood that they thought they were better than the people of the south. We were not only abeed, black slaves, we were "infidels," inferiors, who could not drink from a Muslim's cup or eat from his plate. Giemma and his family had made my life miserable, but they did not seem to care. They did not understand how I hated my life with them.

Over the years I had learned much living with Giemma's family, but the most important thing I learned was that no one could see what went on inside your head and heart. I had always played a double game with Giemma: I did one thing and thought about another. But at age fourteen, having survived two attempted escapes and planning my next one, I now consciously understood that I was playing this double game. I may have been a slave, but I was free to plan my escape. Giemma was not as smart as he thought. He trusted me, but I did not trust him.

I had learned that these people could change their mind at any time—and kill me. For seven years his wife had hated me. Would Giemma be able to resist forever his wife's pleas to kill me? Or, one night while Giemma was away on business or off on another raid with the militia, would she sneak down to where I slept and kill me herself?

I turned fifteen and then sixteen and then seventeen. I was now taller than Giemma. I had been taking long walks for years, and could walk, even run for hours without tiring. My body was strong and so was my mind.

To this family, I was their black slave, the lowest of the low. To Giemma, I was his most reliable workhorse. In my own mind, however, I was sure that I had finally become the man my father dreamed I would be: I was *muycharko*. Giemma Abdullah and his cruel family had no idea that they had turned a scared little Dinka boy into "twelve men."

Three years had passed since I had been caught escaping. I had now been with Giemma for a total of ten rainy and ten dry seasons—ten years! "It is time to try to leave again," I said to myself. "I don't care what happens. I have to try."

That night I made my plans: This time, I would not go along the road. Instead, I would stay out of sight in the forest, using the road as my guide. My plan was to leave first thing in the morning and get to the nearby market town of Mutari before the sun went down. I had never been to Mutari, but Giemma went there all the time. It was a large market town with many people, maybe some who would help me. I now knew which road he took.

"God," I said. "This is the final try. I will either make it, or it will be the end of my life. Please help me."

I promised myself—and God—that this time I would not give up. If someone caught me, I vowed to tell them to kill me. I would fight them to make sure they killed me, because I could not be a slave again. And if they didn't kill me, I would kill myself. I refused to live as a slave any longer.

"Please, God, don't let me be hurt or killed. Don't let me die."

The next morning I headed out with the cows as usual, bringing them to a familiar area near the Mutari road. As soon as they started grazing, I ran as fast as I could for as long as I could through the wood along the road toward Mutari. For hours.

No one stopped me. The day was passing, the sun was dropping in the sky, and I was farther away from Giemma's than I had ever been on my own in ten years. I was hot and tired and dirty, but I felt a relief and then a kind of excitement that I allowed myself to enjoy. That night would be my first out of Giemma's control. Before the sun went down I arrived in Mutari, the biggest town in the area, where people came from every village to buy and sell. I was out of Giemma's reach. I knew it would be difficult for him to find me. Within a matter of hours I had put ten years behind me. I knew I could do it, and I did! I was walking in this new town, lined with streets of one-story buildings made of mud with straw roofs, and no one knew what I had done. I saw other Dinka working with their masters, and no one seemed to suspect that I had escaped from mine. I was so happy, and I allowed myself to enjoy this strange new feeling of being on my own, being responsible for my own choices. I was free!

But soon I got nervous. I had made it to Mutari, but where would I spend the night? Who would help me? I decided that I should go to the local police. For years I had heard Giemma and his neighbors mention the *bolis*–men who settled disputes over property and cattle. If there were fights, someone would call the police. I knew the police solved problems and helped people, and I needed help. I asked people on the street for directions to the police, and I made my way to a one-story building of mud with a straw roof, just like most of the other buildings in Mutari, and went inside.

An Arab man dressed in the green shirt and trousers of the Sudanese police was sitting at a desk. He seemed surprised by my arrival. I had never spoken to a policeman before. (For ten years I had spoken to few people other than Giemma and his family.) But for years, I had been thinking about what I would say to someone once I escaped Giemma, and the words came out.

"I need help," I said, and he took me to another man, who asked me my problem, and I told him that I had been living with this family since I was seven, didn't like the way they treated me, and I didn't want to be with them anymore. I had escaped.

"I want to find some people from the south who could help me," I told him. I was worried that the man I had escaped from would come and find me.

"We'll talk to you later," he said, sending me to a waiting area where others were sitting. I sat down. He left without saying a word. I waited. No one talked to me. The other people in the room were called away, new people arrived. And I just waited. After a few hours, I was the only person waiting. But what else could I do? Where could I go? I needed help, and who else would help me in this big, strange town?

Finally, a policeman came and told me to follow him. He took me to a kitchen area where they were preparing the evening meal. "Clean up," he said, and showed me what needed to be done.

For the next two months, I worked for the Mutari police. I was their kitchen boy. They fed me, and I worked. I went to the police to get help because I had been enslaved, and the police made me their slave. I slept in a corner of the kitchen.

I did not question them. If this was their idea of helping me, I accepted it. Initially, I expected that any day they would deal with my problem. When I finally realized they had no intention of helping me, whom could I complain to? I had told my story, and these men with guns in their holsters made me their slave. After two days working in the kitchen, a policeman took me outside and showed me two donkeys with large jugs slung over them. We took the donkeys to a nearby watering hole where he ordered me to fill up the jugs. This was my new job—to carry water to the police station. Every morning someone woke me up, and I led the donkeys to the watering place, filled the tanks and brought them back to the station. I refilled the tanks several times a day and brought them back to the station. I also cleaned the kitchen and washed dishes for them. For ten years, Giemma had forced me to work for him, and I escaped only to be forced by the police to do their dirty work.

I did not intend to escape one kind of slavery for another. One Thursday afternoon, the first of the two big market days in Mutari, I took one of the donkeys from the police station. Instead of going after the water, I led the animal into the main marketplace, tied him up, and walked into the crowd.

CHAPTER NINE

AN ACT OF KINDNESS— AND ANOTHER

On the edge of the main market in Mutari was an area where the trucks loaded and unloaded their goods. I had noticed these trucks before, and hoped that one of them would be my ride out of Mutari and away from slavery forever. I saw a man supervising two boys loading boxes on one of the trucks.

"I want to go to another town," I said.

"What town?" he asked.

I didn't know, didn't even care. I told him I was looking for people I knew.

I told him my story, how I had been taken when I was seven to work for a family and escaped from them after ten years. He listened to me, and he looked at me, and I was sure he was not going to help me. His truck was piled with bulging burlap sacks, and his workers were ready to go.

He told me he was heading for ed-Da'ein, his hometown.

"Please take me with you," I said.

"It's a dangerous place for you," he said. "Lots of militia there." He told me that ed-Da'ein was a Rizeigat town, filled with members of the same militia group many of Giemma's neighbors belonged to. The Rizeigat had been raiding Dinka areas a few hundred miles to the south—my region—and bringing slaves back to ed-Da'ein. Shaking his head at the horror of the memory, he told me that, ten years before, a lot of people from southern Sudan had been killed in ed-Da'ein. They had run into a church to escape the militia, who proceeded to set the church on fire to smoke them out. They refused to come out—and were burned alive inside the church.

"It's a dangerous place," he said again, as if to make sure I understood. And I did: People who looked like me could get murdered in this town I was asking him to take me to. Ten years ago—about the same time I was kidnapped on that day the militia killed all those people in Nyamlell—the *murahaliin* also killed those people in the church. I thought of those people on fire inside, with no place to go, screaming, but knowing that if they ran out of the church the militiamen would shoot them down. They chose to die in the church. Why did the Arab people want to murder the Dinka?[2]

But I did not ask him that. I asked him if there were still Dinka people in ed-Da'ein. Maybe I would know someone.

"Will you take me?"

He nodded. "Get in," he said. At first I didn't understand him. "In there," he told me, and pointed to a place in the back

---

[2] In 1987, about 2,000 displaced Dinka, afraid they were going to be attacked by Arab militiamen, went to a police station in ed-Da'ein for protection. The police advised the refugees to spend the night in nearby railroad freight cars (not a church, as the truck driver had said), and they did. The Dinka were attacked by militia, shot, and burned to death—while the police watched. See *Human Rights Abuses in Sudan, 1987: The ed-Da'ein Massacre,* Ushari Mahmud and Suliman Baldo (Khartoum, 1987).

of his truck between the burlap sacks, where no one could see me. The driver helped me climb in and hide behind his cargo, the two kids climbed on top, he stepped into the driver's seat, and we headed out of Mutari. Sitting amidst his cargo, which smelled like onions and grain, my body buzzed with excitement: I was leaving Mutari to find some people I knew.

The truck stopped a couple of times at rest stops for gas and food. The driver—his name was Abdah—told me to join them for something to eat. I was afraid to get out and waited nervously for them to return. Abdah brought me something to eat. After a two hours on the road, sometime after midnight, we arrived in a truck depot.

Ed-Da'ein was the biggest place I had ever seen, much bigger than Mutari, with more buildings. I felt that familiar combination of excitement and fear. Abdah invited me to come home with him. Immediately, a warning flashed in my mind: *"He wants to make you work for him!"* That's what people in the north did with people like me. First Giemma and his neighbors, then the police, and now this truck driver wanted to use me.

"No," I said. He read the fear on my face.

"Don't worry," Abdah assured me. "I want to help you—otherwise I never would have allowed you to get into my truck. I will protect you. If you want to be safe, if you want to find your parents some day, you cannot stay here on your own. These people hate your people, they hate you. Come to my home."

He explained that his work took him to many different places, and ed-Da'ein, his own hometown, was the most dangerous. "Bad things can happen to you here—worse than anything in the place you escaped from," he warned me. He remembered the smell that day the people were burned not far from where he lived. He was worried about leaving me on my own in ed-Da'ein, and his worries quickly infected me. What would I do, now that I was there? I had to get away from Giemma and the police in Mutari. But now that I was in ed-Da'ein, a center of the Rizeigat murahaliin, where would I go?

He assured me that no one would bother me at his house.

"We'll find a way to get you to the capital," he said. "You will find many South Sudanese there, maybe your family. But you must come with me."

I was confused and nervous. I had two dangers to choose from: this new place where they roast Dinka people alive, or this new man, who might enslave me. I began crying. The tears came so quickly I could not stop them.

"Don't worry," he said with a measure of kindness in his voice that I had never heard from the mouth of an Arab person. "I want you to be safe."

I decided to try him. I had escaped from Giemma and the police; I could escape from Abdah. God was protecting me.

He took me to his house and then went to talk to his wife to explain that I was going to stay with them. Then she came out and said, "Hello." I thanked her. Abdah stressed that she could not let anyone know that I was with them. She agreed and left.

When I heard her welcome and his warning to keep my presence a secret I was very happy. I was proud that I had found such a kind truck driver who would take me home to his wife, a woman who would welcome me. The only other Muslim woman I had known was Giemma's wife, and every time she talked to me she said she preferred me dead.

I liked Abdah and his wife, but still feared that they might try to do something. Though my heart told me that these

Muslims were kind people, my head—and my history—told me to watch out.

For the next two months I lived with them and their two little boys. His wife fed me with the same food she prepared for her husband and children. They treated me as if I were a visiting friend or relative. I no longer worried that they would try to take advantage of me. I told Abdah how his own people had enslaved me, and he shook his head. "It is a bad situation," he said, even admitting that he knew people who had gone to the south and taken slaves. For some people, he explained, slavery was "a business." He himself, however, did not believe in making another person work without pay, and I did not have to worry about him forcing me to work for him.

"I want to help you find your people and your parents," he said. Listening to Abdah and living with his family for several weeks, I realized that not all Muslims were like Giemma and his neighbors, that there were some like Abdah and his wife, who, even though they lived among the most notorious raiders of Dinkaland, believed that no Muslim had the right to enslave other human beings.

It turned out that Abdah would not be going to Khartoum any time soon. He asked some friends whether they could help me get a ride, but from the way he described things, I knew that I had to be very careful; there were only so many people he could trust, and even they were not willing to take a chance of driving a young, escaped slave out of ed-Da'ein, the town filled with Rizeigat raiders. Abdah had told me that this was a dangerous place, and I believed him. I had become an expert in danger. Danger was something that I respected. When Abdah warned me that if I left his house during the day I would risk being abducted again, I believed him. I stayed inside and waited for him to tell me what to do next.

"The bus is the only way," Abdah announced one day. "You must take the bus to Khartoum."

"I have no money for the ticket," I said.

"I will buy you the ticket," said Abdah.

The bus was not really a bus, but a truck. The passengers rode in a seating area in the back, their bags stored underneath. Arab people and Africans from eastern Sudan known as the *Fur*—people whose skin was darker than the Dinka, but who were Muslim—had come to ed-Da'ein from all over the region to travel to the capital. I was the only Dinka.

The trip to the capital—the local people generally referred to Khartoum as "the capital"—took almost three days. I kept to myself, lost in the excitement that I might find my parents, or at least get some news of them.

In the late afternoon, with the sun still in the sky, the bus pulled up to a place filled with other buses, the main station in Khartoum. Everyone got off the bus. Some were greeted by friends and family. My fellow passengers got their bags and left. I had nothing but the clothes I was wearing, and no one was waiting for me. Abdah had given me a ticket and ten Sudanese pounds, which I had spent on food during the trip.

The station was packed with people. I saw an empty bench and sat down to think about what to do next. I looked around at all the people, none of whom looked at me. I saw some Africans, even people who looked like they might be Dinka. But everyone was rushing someplace. Only I had no place to go. My head filled with thoughts: I had made it to the capital. From Giemma's land in Kerio, I had run to Mutari, where I had escaped from the police, and then, in Abdah's truck, I had traveled to ed-Da'ein, and now I was sitting in the main bus station of the capital city of all of Sudan, Khartoum. I had traveled very far. It was like a dream. During my stay with Abdah's family, my mind had relaxed a bit. Now my mind was racing again at high gear. What next?

There seemed to be fewer people in the station. It was now dark, and about four hours had passed, but I still had no clear idea of what to do, now that I was in Khartoum. I was tired and hungry and dirty. As I focused on the problem of where I would sleep that night, I noticed a man walk by me—a tall, black man, an African. He looked at me, I looked at him, and he kept walking. Abdah had said there were many Dinka in Khartoum. Was that man Dinka?

I began thinking about how I might find where my people lived in this city, and then the man returned and was speaking to me in Arabic.

"Which tribe are you from?" he asked.

"Dinka."

He smiled at me. "I am Dinka, too. It's late, why are you sitting here?" I told him that I had traveled from ed-Da'ein, and I didn't know where to go.

"That's what I thought." He explained that when he first saw me sitting alone, dirty and with ragged clothes, he assumed I was just another one of the street kids in the capital, hanging out in the bus station, hoping for a handout. At that time of the evening most of the refugees who had jobs in Khartoum had returned to the camps where they lived, hours away on the outskirts of the city. But as he headed for his bus it occurred to him that maybe I was a new refugee, one of his people. He decided to find out.

I told him I had come to Khartoum, hoping to find someone who would take me to where people from the south live.

"I am going there now," he said. He explained that he usually took a bus from another station but had missed it and had come to the main station to catch another bus to the camp where he lived. He asked me what part of the south I was from.

"Aweil," I said.

He smiled again. He was from an area of the south that was even closer to the Arab border than my village, but there were many people from Aweil and the rest of the Bahr al-Ghazal area of southern Sudan in another camp. "Maybe you will find someone you know," he said.

I told him that I did not have any money for a ticket.

He shrugged. "Come with me," he said, heading for the bus to this camp where I would meet people from my homeland. I hustled after him, my head now bubbling with thoughts of seeing my family again. He pointed to an area where many other Dinka people were standing. The bus from this station would take me to another in a place called Souq-Libya, a market town ("souq" means market) where I would change for another bus that would take me directly to the camp he had told me about, the place they called "Jabarona."

"The people will help you," he said, gesturing to the Dinka waiting for the next bus to Souq-Libya. "They all live in Jabarona."

The name surprised me. In Arabic, "jabarona" meant "the forced place." It seemed a strange name for a town—the place we are forced to be.

CHAPTER TEN

JABARONA

Five million people live in Khartoum. Within a matter of weeks I had gone from Giemma's farm to Mutari, a market town that seemed like a city to me, to a real city, the capital of Sudan, which is the largest country in Africa. It was a lot to take in, especially for a boy who had been living inside his head for ten years. As fascinating as the sights of Khartoum were, I found myself preoccupied with my feelings, which moved between excitement and fear and hope without ever stopping long in one of those places.

I believed that God was with me, and so was a little luck: My prayers had finally been answered, and I escaped Giemma without getting caught; I had met Abdah, a kind Muslim who had rescued me in Mutari and then bought me a bus ticket to Khartoum, and now in the capital, I had been rescued again by a Dinka man who also put me on a bus—this time one filled with other Dinka. I was in a large, strange, frightening Muslim city. But I was alive, free, and for the first time since I was a small child, I felt safe. In fact, sitting on that bus with all those members of my own tribe, heading to a place where there were thousands more, I felt great.

As the bus left the station and headed out through the
dusty streets of the capital, I stared out the window at the lights
of the vehicles stirring up the dust of the main streets. I had
never seen so much light in the darkness. There seemed to be
street after street of tall buildings. At a time of night when
country people were already in bed, people were still walking
the streets of Khartoum, while others sat at tables, eating in
restaurants prettier than the places I had seen in Mutari and
ed-Da'ein. I wondered what it would be like to have someone
feed me a beautiful, expensive meal in such a place. But
instead of good food, I was smelling something strange in the
air, which I later realized was the stench of the diesel fumes
coming from my bus and virtually every other vehicle on the
streets of Khartoum.

I turned to the Dinka man next to me and asked him how I
could find people from the Aweil area. He assured me that there
were many from Aweil in the camp, and asked my name and
what area I was from: "Who was your chief?" I told him that I
was Francis Piol Bul Buk. His face registered recognition. Piol
was a famous name among the Malwal Dinka; he knew people
from the clan where many people had the name "Piol," Dinka
for rain. I explained that I had been away from my family for
many years, but I remembered our chief's name—Arop Kuot.

He nodded. Everyone from Aweil knew this chief. When
we got to the camp he promised to bring me to a man from
Aweil who had other Piols in his family. This man would help
me. I thanked him and sat back in my seat enjoying a strange
feeling, one that I had not felt since before I was captured.
Thinking back, I now recognize that feeling was a sense of

confidence that things were going to get better for me. Until
that moment, fear had dominated my life for a decade: fear of
a beating, fear of injury, fear of sickness, fear of responsibility,
fear of death, fear of fear. My little world had been surrounded
by fear, hemmed in by fear.

I have often wondered why such a fearful life did not make
me crazy, or at least cripple me into a state of inaction. But I
never lost hope. And while the thought of escaping and freedom was not on my mind every minute of every day, it never
left my mind. My dream of getting away and finding my family was what kept me working, playing my double game, building Giemma's trust and dependence on me so that one day I
could run away. For the first time in a decade, I felt relaxed and
understood why.

The bus stopped, and I looked out the window. We had
arrived at the bus station in a large town. It was Souq-Libya,
where I would change for the bus to Jabarona. I followed the
other riders to a nearby bus and climbed aboard. As it headed
out of the station, I looked out the window and got lost in the
lights streaming by outside and my thoughts of finding some
familiar faces in this Jabarona. I had succeeded in running
away. It had taken much strength—mental power mainly. For
years I had told myself that I was not a mere, skinny, scared
Dinka boy, a miserable black slave. I was really muycharko.
Sitting on that bus surrounded by black faces like mine, heading to a place where there would be thousands more of my
people, and leaving my life with Giemma Abdullah miles
behind for good, I began to believe that my father had been
right: I was really "twelve men."

"We are here," said my new friend. It had been a long

trip, many hours, and it was now late at night. Where would I sleep? We got off the bus and I looked around. Every time I stepped out of a vehicle I saw something I had never seen before: the city of ed-Da'ein, the even bigger city of Khartoum, the capital, and now Jabarona, a settlement of tin shacks, straw huts, and lean-tos. No trees, no bushes—just these small buildings, more than I could count, stretching for miles and miles, their fires flickering in the dark. My co-rider told me that thousands and thousands of our people lived in places like this in the desert, hours outside the capital and Omduran, Khartoum's sister city across the Nile. The refugees from the south had been pouring into this area for ten years, literally millions of people, mainly Dinka, but also people escaping fighting in eastern Sudan, those people we called the Fur, who, even though they were Muslims, were under attack by the government.

I was never happier to arrive in any place in my life. For the first time since I had been packed on that donkey in Nyamlell, I was surrounded by my people, and we were not forbidden to talk to each other. It was not home, though it felt like home and it smelled like home. We walked through the unpaved streets of the camp, one hut looking like the next. It was late at night, but the camp was like a city, filled with people talking and yelling, little kids running around, some in shorts, others naked, playing in the dirt, the air filled with the smells of fires and food.

Jabarona was crowded and dirty and noisy, without electricity or proper water supplies, buzzing with flies and big mosquitoes. Men yelled at each other. Others weaved along the street too drunk to make a straight line. If the glass and metal littering the roads did not cut your feet, the rocks sticking from the ground would punish them. People seemed to throw their garbage everywhere. The wind blew hard through the area, stirring up sand and threatening to knock down the flimsy houses.

To this Dinka boy who had been enslaved for ten years and on the run for months, dirty, fly-infested Jabarona—the place we are forced to be—was the most beautiful place in the world.

My guide pointed to a shack that looked like every other. "Wait outside," he said, and went into the house. A few minutes later he emerged with another man, who looked like he had been sleeping. I was introduced to Garang, an older man of about fifty, very strong looking but more than a head shorter than I was. He asked me what tribe I was from.

"Dinka Malwal," I told him.

Garang asked me what area of Malwal was I from, and I told him that I had been born in Aweil province, in the village of Gourion.

"I know Gourion," he said.

I cannot even describe the feeling I had when he said "Gourion," the name of my town. I had said that name to myself many times over the past ten years, as if to remind myself that it really existed. The joy of hearing another person say "Gourion"—another Dinka from Aweil!—ran through my entire body. For ten years I had been with people who did not speak my language. For ten years, every time I ate their food I was reminded that I was living in a culture different from my family's. And now God had blessed me: I was among my own people. When I told him my name—Piol Bol Buk—he smiled. We were members of the same clan. He, too, had relatives who were "Piols." He explained that our people were famous among the Dinka of Aweil because, many, many years before—a hundred years ago—one of my ancestors had "talked to the rain" and brought water from the clouds to end a long dry season. I had never heard that story.

I was even happier now, and proud. For the first time since I was captured I was with my own clan, the kind of people whom we Dinka call "uncle" and "cousin." Though we were not kin by blood, Garang and I had ancestors in common. He would show me the kind of hospitality that my own father's brother would. Garang's wife and children were asleep. He offered me something to eat, and asked me questions about my family. I told him what happened to me, how I had not seen my parents since that day ten years ago. He shook his head with sadness. He had heard this story before.

"Have you seen my family?" I asked.

"No," Garang said. "They're not here in Jabarona." He said he knew all the people from Aweil in Jabarona, and certainly all those who were members of our clan.

"Maybe they are in one of the other camps," he said, keeping my hopes alive. Though it was true that most of the refugees from Aweil had ended up in Jabarona, Aweil people also lived in the other camps. I could visit them and ask around; maybe I would find someone who knew my parents or other people from Gourion.

"But it is now time for us to get some rest," he said, showing me where I could sleep in a corner of his small house.

When I awoke the next morning, he introduced me to his wife and three children. I soon discovered that three other young men from Aweil without families were staying there. I wanted to talk to everyone, but the words came with difficulty. Surrounded by so many Dinka and the sounds of the Dinka dialects, I realized that, after ten years of speaking Arabic, my own language was rusty. More upsetting to me was that the Dinka I remembered was really the language of a seven-year-old boy. I had trouble following conversations. The words came at me so quickly, and while I nodded at their familiarity, I didn't always know what they meant. Sometimes I would understand what someone said only long after he had stopped speaking. The meaning would sneak up on me and announce itself. I realized I would have to learn my own language. But that could wait. Garang's wife cooked me a meal the Dinka way, boiled chicken covered with corn sauce. I ate my food and thought of my mother.

In a refugee camp everyone has a story. Since my escape, I had been telling my story to other people, and now at Jabarona I heard many new stories. I had been captured in a murahaliin raid in Nyamlell, and I quickly learned that most of the people in Jabarona had been victims of similar violent attacks, an amazing number of them in Nyamlell, a regular source, I now learned, of cattle and slaves for the militia.

I really had no idea why such a terrible thing had happened to me and my friends. As a little boy, I knew that Arab people lived in my country; I had seen these lighter-skinned people in the market place, in their djellabahs, selling sugar and tea. I had also heard people talking about "wars" and about the murahaliin. But now in Jabarona I heard about the war between the Arabs of northern Sudan and my people in the south, which had been going on longer than I had been alive. For the first time in my life I was learning the story of my people and their history, and it was more powerful than anything they teach you in school, because I had lived this story, and so had all the people in this camp.

I had been taken away from Nyamlell in 1986, and I now learned that what happened to that little boy had also happened to millions of other Dinka in the south. The proof was all around me. In the first few days I was in Jabarona, I talked to many people from my region about the violence against our people. I learned that in 1986 the militia staged several raids in the area and continued to attack Nyamlell and surrounding villages every dry season for the next fifteen years. My native area was only about fifty miles below the border, and therefore an easy target for raiders. They would ride into Dinkaland on their horses, camels, donkeys, even in Toyota pickup trucks, shoot up several small villages, kill the men, and ride off with the women, the children, and even more important to the murahaliin, Dinka cattle.

"Why didn't the police or the government stop them?" I asked. People laughed at me: the government supported the raids. The army protected the *murahaliin*. People had reported that in recent raids on Nyamlell the militia were riding in government armored vehicles. The men who escaped the militia's machine gun bullets and the women or children who fled into the bush would return to their smoking villages to find mango trees chopped down and their property destroyed. Sometimes the militia would burn the nearby papyrus fields, the main material for Dinka roofs. Without their animals, without their fields, without their men, women, and children, without roofs over their heads, how could the people survive? These raids and the civil war had left millions of Dinka dead and driven millions more to the north, searching for safety in the shanty-towns and in the camps outside of Khartoum—which the government called "peace camps."

Everyone in the camps was looking for somebody: their relatives, their children, their brothers or sisters, and, like me, their parents. When the raiders had rushed into their villages shooting and slashing, the people ran in every direction to save their own lives. Years later, they had no idea whether their neighbors or family members were killed, enslaved, or living in a refugee camp in Kenya, or here in the capital.

I hoped my family made it to Khartoum. For several days after my arrival I talked to as many people as I could in Jabarona to find out some news about my family. I told people what had happened to me, how I had been enslaved for ten years and escaped. Most people I met were reluctant to talk about what happened to them. It was upsetting, of course. But everyone had pretty much the same story, and others were unlikely to be impressed. My story, however, was all I had with me, the only remnant of my past. I told them my story. I was also full of opinions, and my main view was that the Sudanese Arabs were doing terrible things to the Sudanese Dinka. I talked to many people, and though I did not meet another person who had been a slave, no one seemed shocked by my story. The Arabs had been taking Dinka slaves for centuries. My people sang songs about slave raids. I quickly learned that slavery was part of Dinka history. When new people arrived in the camp, I visited them and asked them whether they had met my family. No one had.

I kept visiting people, people came to see me, I kept talking to everyone.

. . .

I talked too much. Eleven days after I arrived in Jabarona, two men came up to me.

"We heard that you are against the government," they said.

I could not believe my ears, for my eyes told me that these were black African men, though not Dinka, dressed like everyone else in the camp.

"You are telling people that you are a slave who has escaped."

Now I was really scared. I knew I was in trouble.

"No," I said. "I am not telling people that."

"Come with us." I looked around me at the other Dinka, and their eyes turned away. I saw Garang, and he shrugged: There was nothing he could do. This was the way of the camps.

"What did I do?" I asked them. "I did nothing wrong."

They repeated the charge: "People have told us that you are saying things against the government," they repeated. I told them that these people are wrong.

"Who are these people?" I had spoken only to Dinka people about my story, and I could not imagine that one of my own people would put the police on me. These men would not tell me the names of the people who had informed on me. They were the police, they said, and I must come with them.

They took me to a police station in Jabarona where I waited for a while, and then they put me in a car.

I remember very little about the drive from Jabarona. My mind was too full of questions and fears. Where were they taking me? What would they do to me? I had tasted freedom for almost three months, I loved being among my people, even in that ugly, noisy, dirty refugee camp. And now I was under arrest.

We arrived in an area on the edge of Khartoum and drove to a big building—a prison. Inside, they handed me over to officials who brought me into a room and made the same accusation that the Jabarona police had: "You have been saying you are an escaped slave; making antigovernment statements."

Again I denied it. So they beat me up. They slapped me and punched me and knocked me down, and when I was down they kicked me in the back and on my sides with their big boots. When they stopped, they ordered me once again to admit to my crimes, and once again I denied that I had done anything wrong.

"We will kill you!" one man yelled at me. I said nothing. My silence enraged them and they kicked me again. I huddled against the floor with nothing to tell them.

They dragged me into a big room filled with twenty or so other men and left me there. The next morning one of the men who beat me up returned again and asked me if I was ready to talk. I said I had nothing to say. I was innocent.

"You are lying!" he said and punched me. "People" had told the police that I was an enemy of the government.

"They are lying," I said.

He revealed a leather whip, the sort I used to use on the cattle (and Giemma used on me), and he beat me with it. He hurt me terribly. But I said nothing.

Every day, for weeks, someone came and asked me if I was ready to confess.

"Did you say you had been a slave?"

I denied that I had ever been a slave.

"Did you escape from your master?"

I claimed that I was a refugee from the south, from raids on my village. I never had a master, I was never a slave. I was a refugee, just like every other Dinka in Khartoum. I lied to these men because, as soon as they started questioning me, I realized why I had been arrested. Someone in the camp had informed on me. I was telling people my story, and someone told the police. At first, I could not believe a Dinka person would do something like that. The people in Jabarona had been so friendly, so eager to help a new refugee. Why would they help the government that was attacking our people? Why would they work for the enemy?

I was able to answer my question myself. Most of the people in the camps were desperately poor. Few had jobs, and most had large families to support. There was so little money that no one ever talked about money. Most people never even talked about what happened to them, unless asked. People talked about food. About water. When will they help us? When would the international workers bring more food to the camps?

Someone had made some money by telling the police about me. Everyone in the camps knew there were informers working for the police. The government had denied that there was any slavery in Sudan, and they were not about to let a seventeen-year-old Dinka boy wander from camp to camp telling everyone he had been a slave for ten years. I had already heard how scared people were to tell the truth to the foreigners who periodically came into the camps to talk to refugees, often meeting secretly to find out what was really happening in Sudan.

"You are a person who is saying bad things about the government," the policeman said to me.

"I don't say anything about the government," I assured him. I was just a refugee.

"You are talking to the Americans, to the UN people," he insisted.

I told him that I had never talked to anyone but Dinka people in the camps. I did not know where this "America" was. And while I had heard people mention this "U–N," I had no idea what it meant. I had been in the camp for only a few days, how could I talk to foreigners?

I was lying, of course. I had told my story to too many people. By now, I knew that many Dinka had managed to be sent to other countries, to "America," to the "U.S." I knew that this UN brought food into the camps and tried to help people. I had heard of something called "The Red Cross," which also brought food and medicine. Whenever anyone said "Americans," they talked of people who helped our people.

"Aren't you afraid to tell your story?" people in the camps would ask me, and I would tell them that it was my story, my life, I had seen all of it, felt all of it. One man even inquired whether, if he could find someone from another country to talk to me, from "America" maybe, I would tell him that I had been taken from my family and made a slave?

"Of course I would tell them," I said. "This was a bad thing they did. This happened to me."

Maybe he was the one who informed on me, maybe he was setting me up, maybe he decided to make some money off my stupidity. The fact was that I could not recall how many people I had told my story to. Any one of them—or several—could have informed on me. The government had waved money in front of very poor people—starving, desperate people—and some could not resist that temptation. Yet, it still hurt me to think that a Dinka might have turned me in to the police. In the world of my parents and my village, the Dinka helped each other; they were not the enemy.

"Dinka people are eating other Dinka," I heard a man say one day. I could not imagine why he would say such a thing.

Sitting through those first days in prison, I now knew what he meant. But I refused to let them eat me. I had told the truth about being a slave, and it got me thrown into jail and tortured. I would continue to lie to the guards, because I knew that telling the truth would certainly get me more pain, and probably get me killed.

After a few days the beatings stopped. *My* beatings anyway. I watched the guards beat newcomers, some resisting, but others telling them what they wanted—even if it was not true. They were dragged away, and I wondered whether the punishment they received was worse than the beating they would have suffered. I saw other prisoners kicked and whipped. I heard stories of torture, of fingernails and toenails torn off to get someone to confess. But I never saw that kind of treatment, and I was never tortured that badly.

My fellow prisoners were a varied group: young men my age, older ones, people from the south, Muslims from the north, from different tribes, crammed together into those large cells, all waiting to be charged with a crime or transferred to a bigger prison. Some were clearly dangerous men, and I kept my distance; others were small-time criminals and thieves, or common troublemakers who had been picked up on the streets for fighting or being drunk. And some were like me—pure amateurs who had somehow gotten on the wrong side of the police, usually for political reasons, and ended up in jail. No one talked much, probably afraid that his neighbor would inform on them for better treatment. For a bunch of prisoners, in fact, we were all quite well behaved. There were no fights. I never saw a prisoner abuse another prisoner.

We spent our days sitting around killing time; we sat in the unlit cell surrounded by darkness and the noise from the other cells. With no toilet in the room, we were required to ask for permission. A guard would accompany several of us, single file, to the latrines where other guards also watched. We had to clean up quickly, and then the guards brought us back to the cell. They gave us food twice a day, but food even worse than what I had eaten on Giemma's farm. Bread and beans, a kind of sandwich, with some water or soda. The only time I saw the light of day was while going to the latrines or when a guard opened the cell to bring in food.

The questions, however, never stopped. It seemed that every morning a man turned up to ask me, "Are you going to tell your story to people?" and "Did you tell them a story about being a slave?"

"No," I insisted. "I never told anyone that."

They were trying every which way to get me to slip up. But I kept denying that I had been a slave. Over and over again I said, "I was never a slave. I do not deserve to be in prison."

I was miserable in that place. All I could think about was how, after ten years of dreaming of freedom, I had escaped from Giemma, and now I was in jail with a bunch of criminals. Jail was even worse than life with Giemma. I could escape him. He would send me into the forest with his cows, and I could run away. In prison, I had no place to run. The constant darkness and the crowded conditions made it a scary place. There were no beds; we slept on the floor with very little space between us. The risk of getting in the way or bumping into a fellow prisoner was great, and the consequences of such an accident were unpredictable. I stayed in my spot. No one seemed to talk about himself, and I certainly was not about to break that rule. My mouth had gotten me hauled off to prison, and I was not about to give anyone else a reason to improve his situation by informing on me. The others complained among themselves about the food and the beatings, and I am sure I joined in. But we all avoided discussing personal matters. I made no friends. One of my strongest memories of those dark days in that prison was restraining my urge to socialize and retreating inside my head for company, just as I had done for years in my little hut near Giemma's animals.

But even in jail I found another dream: "When I get released, I will do everything I can to escape from this country, my country, Sudan," I told myself.

I now realized that I would never be safe in my country. I had felt comfortable and safe in Jabarona, but I was wrong to feel that way. I saw bad things happen in that camp, I had heard of even worse things: people were arrested for no reason. And then it happened to me.

I also realized that even if I found my family in Khartoum I still would not be safe. We would not be safe. There was a war, there was hatred between the Muslims and my people, to them we Dinka were all "abeed." They had no respect for us. They shot us down and carved us up like wild animals. For twenty years this craziness had gone on, and no end was in sight. More refugees arrived in the camps every day. It would never get better. Once I was released from jail, I had to leave the country.

It never occurred to me that I would not be released. Why?

I had already survived so much; I would survive again. They did not seem to have any hard proof that I was a slave. Otherwise, why would they keep asking me if I said it? I knew I would get out of there—just as I knew I would get away from Giemma Abdullah.

God was at my back.

CHAPTER ELEVEN

THE PROCESS

Seven months later I was still in that jail. The days dragged by. Having spent the past ten years of my life working from sunup to sundown, I had never known that one day could last so long. Hard men lived with me in that place, but I kept to myself, I kept quiet, and I was left alone. I also began to worry that I might never get out of prison.

No one had come to visit me.

And then I was released. I was never sure why. It had something to do with the charges. The police had no real evidence against me, other than the report from the informer that I had claimed I was a slave. I had denied that charge, and it was the word of one abd against another, and perhaps that is not enough to keep a man in jail in Khartoum. (Though I had heard that men were arrested and even killed routinely for less evidence.) But, as flimsy as the charges were against me, other inmates were also released in what must have been some kind of end-of-year general amnesty for prisoners who had not yet been charged with a specific crime or had not gone to trial.

"Tomorrow you will be released," a guard told us one day

in September. The announcement came as such a total shock to us prisoners that we took it as some kind of cruel joke. But then the next day, when the sun was at its highest in the sky, we were all let go. The only explanation we got was that the leader of Sudan had "forgiven us." Before we were officially released, an official met with each prisoner. He said to me, "You will not say bad things about the government again." I assured him that would be so, thanked him for letting me go, and then I walked out of the prison gate.

Suddenly I was free again. I could not believe my good luck. But I had not forgotten the promise I made to myself during my seven months of imprisonment: I would now devote myself to doing everything I could to get out of this country. I had been a victim of abduction by force, I had been a slave, I had been a refugee, and now I was also an ex-prisoner. It was too much life for a seventeen-year-old. I wanted something better for myself. I had experienced the relief of freedom, but I now realized that the happiness, the relaxation I felt in the camp—which was really the absence of the anxiety of my life under Giemma and then on the run—was a false sense of security. I now knew that for any Dinka living in Sudan, there was always an automatic weapon waiting to go off, or a sword about to fall, or a government informer earning his pay by sending another man to prison.

I would leave Sudan. Of course, I had not forgotten my efforts to find news of my family. I set myself two jobs for the next several months: to find out as much as I could about the fate of my family, and to get the papers I needed that would allow me to go north to Egypt.

In the short time I had been in Jabarona and then again in

prison, I had heard about people who got their "visa" to Cairo. "They're going to Cairo," people would say. "They've got their papers and are leaving for Cairo." There were also stories about people who had gone to Cairo and were now living in America—a place people talked about, though I had no idea where it was. I also heard about the UN, which helped Dinka go to England, Australia, and Canada, as well as America. For me, these were meaningless names of places I had never even heard of before I had arrived in Khartoum. The key was "the process." People said, "You have to go through the process," and then you could go to Cairo. I knew no more about Egypt or Cairo than I did about America, Canada, Australia, or England—except that I, too, wanted to go there as soon as I got out of prison.

"How do you go to Cairo?" That was the first thing I said to Garang when I returned to Jabarona on that miraculous day I was released from prison. Although I was still angry that someone in the camp had put the secret police onto me, I had no place else to go. I also knew it was possible to begin "the process" in Jabarona. And so I returned to Garang's house and they welcomed me. I swallowed my anger over no one visiting me in prison. Everyone in Jabarona was scared of government reprisals; no one wanted to be the next victim of the secret police. Garang and his family would not want to risk being identified as a close friend of an "enemy of the government" like me.

It was comforting, though, to find out that people had worried about my fate. Garang was concerned that they might force me into the army. Everyone knew stories about Dinka boys who had been trained as soldiers and then sent south to fight against their own people. My friends from the camp had been sure that they would never see me again.

I saw no future for me in Jabarona. There were no jobs there, and very few Dinka were able to find work in Khartoum. Why would the Muslims of Khartoum hire a Dinka to work, when they could get a slave? Garang knew the world of the camps as well as anyone I had met in Khartoum, and I sought his help.

"There are people in Khartoum," he said. You often heard this in the camps, about "people in the capital," who were "doing things." Pressing him further, I learned that there were Dinka "working in the underground"—what Garang also called "the black market"—to help fellow tribesmen get Sudanese passports and then a visa to Egypt.

Such things required money, of course. I soon learned that you could get almost anything in Khartoum if you had the money. "Doing things" usually meant illegal things, but the right amount of Sudanese pounds could get what you wanted: nice clothes, shoes, fancy watches, food—you name it. People who had money for those luxuries were themselves probably operating in this underground economy. Garang said he had "a friend" in an official position in the Egyptian consulate, a Dinka who would be able to get me a visa. He was famous in the refugee camps for helping people get to Egypt. The price was about two hundred Sudanese pounds, seventy dollars at the 1997 exchange rate.

I did not even have one Sudanese pound. But I told Garang that I had to leave Sudan, that it was too dangerous for me there. One of the truly wonderful traits of the Dinka people is their generosity. It is a custom among my people to help others, and Garang decided that he would help me by raising money in the camp so that I could begin "the process."

Why were they so eager to help me, considering that there were literally millions of Dinka in Khartoum desperate for help? I now realize that I had several things in my favor:

1) I was young and without a family. Dinka people marry young and quickly have large families. It was easier to raise money for one young man to leave than for a family of four or five, and many families in the camp were twice that number.

2) Many refugees did not want to leave Sudan. They were hoping to go back home eventually. Many, like me, were searching for lost family members. Others were afraid to go to another country with strange customs and a new language.

3) I was eager to leave and told everyone how much I wanted to get out of Sudan. As much as I wanted to find my parents, my hopes of doing so were failing.

4) I was an ex-slave. People in Jabarona had heard of this fate, feared it themselves, and for me to have survived such an ordeal turned me into a minor celebrity of sorts among the refugees from Aweil.

I was amazed by the generosity of Garang's neighbors and friends. My friends. I had told them that I wanted to do more with my life, help my people, and, as poor as they were, they wanted to help me. I still hoped that my parents were alive. After all, in spite of the raids and the slaughter in the south, millions of Dinka people and other tribes had survived. The evidence was all around me in the camps. But millions had also died, and I began to deal with the possibility that my own family had perished with them. The people of Jabarona had lost family and friends. Many had seen them slaughtered or burned alive. Why should I be any different? Then again, I had been lucky enough to survive a militia attack. God had helped me escape slavery. Maybe He had spared my parents, too.

But if my family had survived, I would be no good to them dead or in prison. At the time I did not think all of this through carefully. While I could not avoid thinking that my family had probably been killed, I could not stop dreaming of seeing them again. Looking back on that time, I know that I was confused and emotionally strained. But I was not stupid: I was an experienced survivor, and from what I had learned about refugee life in Khartoum over the past seven months, the odds on a young escaped slave surviving—particularly one with a tendency to tell the truth about what had happened to him to anyone who asked—were not good.

I welcomed all the help my kind clansmen in Jabarona offered me. And the money. All I had to do was wait.

My dream was to go to Cairo, but when I did I wanted to go as a Dinka Malwal. That was my tribe, and by birth I was Dinka Malwal. Because I lost my childhood, I was never initiated into my tribe. In fact, I was not officially a man. That initiation happened as early as age sixteen, and I was now almost nineteen. I had no doubt that I was already a man. But I wanted to let the world know I was Dinka Malwal, and that required the tribal markings to be scarred onto my forehead. I sat for the procedure in Jabarona. An expert was found, my forehead was shaved, and with his knife he carved the lines of the Dinka Malwal on my forehead. I could feel the cold of the knife and then the pain. I didn't care. The pain would stop, the blood would dry, the cuts would heal. The important thing was that when I arrived in Cairo, other Dinka would know who I was.

"You need a picture for your passport and visa," Garang informed me. "Several pictures."

I had never had my picture taken. But if this was a necessary part of "the process" to flee Sudan, I would do it. Garang explained that getting photographs did not hurt; in fact, it would be the easiest part of the process.

He took me to the Dar-es-Salaam refugee camp, about a forty-five minute walk away. Filled with refugees from other south Sudanese tribes—Nuba, the Fur, and other lighter skinned Muslim Africans who had better relations with the Arabs—Dar-es-Salaam was a more prosperous place than where we lived, with better houses and more shops and businesses. Garang led me to a small studio where my picture was taken by a black man from eastern Sudan, a Muslim. He placed a clip-on tie around my neck. Garang explained that I had to look good in this picture, because it would appear on my passport, and told me to look at the man and his camera.

"Smile!" he said, and I smiled, even though I did not have anything to smile about. The photographer took several more shots. Garang paid him.

Two days later I returned to the Dar-el-Salaam photo studio, and there, on this shiny piece of paper, was me—smiling back at me. It was strange to see myself for the first time as others saw me. I liked the way I looked, even with the funny tie. Everyone agreed it was a good picture.

"*Francis Fioul Bul Bok.*" When my passport magically appeared from the black market, my name was misspelled. They got "Francis" and "Bul" right, but someone had put "Fioul" instead of "Piol," and "Bok" instead of "Buk."

When Garang handed me the green Sudanese passport with my picture inside and all the official Arabic writing that informed the rest of the world that "Francis Fioul Bul Bok" was a citizen of Sudan, I noticed immediately that they had gotten my name wrong. Garang had told me that it was important to be able to sign my name to my passport and visa, and I had spent a lot of time practicing writing my own name. This passport was the first time I had ever seen my name printed— and it was not my name! I was very upset. I thought, "They won't let me leave Cairo under a wrong name."

"It doesn't matter," Garang assured me. For the authorities, Sudanese and Egyptian, I was my passport. With this name went my picture. My "identity" was now Francis Bok. "You will be able to change it back later," he said, and that made me feel better. I had lost my parents, my village, and I would soon be losing my country. I did not want to go into the strange world of Egypt and maybe beyond without my real name.

Of course, this passport was as phony as my name, and totally illegal. But what else can a refugee do, particularly one who was kidnapped at age seven? I had no birth certificate, or any other kind of proof that I had actually been born in Sudan. I did not even have a witness that I had lived in Sudan, except Giemma Abdullah, and I was not about to submit his name as a reference.

So, on January 28, 1998, I was born again—as Francis Bok. It cost eighty Sudanese pounds.

The next step was to get my visa to Egypt. Garang took my passport and more photos of me and headed back into the black market. He turned over the passport and photos to his friend in the Egyptian consulate. It would take time, and time moved very slowly in Jabarona, where few had jobs or anything else to do. I renewed my search for news about my family. I had heard about another camp not far away from Jabarona, a place called Mawela, and I went there. I also went to Haj-Jusef, and there, too, I found thousands of Dinka, but not one person I knew or who knew me or members of my family. And then one day, in one of the camps (I now forget which) I met a man who looked at me and then said, "I knew your father." I was stunned. The man standing before me knew my father! It was as if someone had told me that I was not crazy; I did have a father, and this man could prove it. But he had met my father many years before, when we still lived in Gourion, before the raids. I would meet other men from different towns in Aweil who had done business with my father. Others told me of having met relatives of mine—people with the name Buk—in other refugee camps. But no one knew anything about my father, mother, or my two sisters. In my mind I saw them as little girls. I realized that baby Achol would be about thirteen years old now. And what had happened to my big brother, who was in a different town that day I was kidnapped? Could all of them be gone?

By the end of March I had my passport back, along with a three-month visa attached to it, allowing Francis Bok, a legal citizen of Sudan, to travel to Egypt. It was like magic. I had no idea how all this paperwork was made to appear out of nothing, and I didn't ask.

I was excited, but I stifled my excitement. I would not permit myself to celebrate until I had crossed the border into Egypt. I would release my pleasure only when I was free of the power of the Sudanese government. And to achieve that I needed a ticket from Khartoum to Cairo.

You did not just go down to the station and buy this ticket. The train was always full. Every week this train left filled with refugees. You had to put your name on a list for a future train. I was told that I had a place in two weeks.

On a day in early April, I was back in the main railroad station in Khartoum boarding the train for the first stage of my journey to Egypt. Once again I had only the clothes on my back. But I did have sixty Egyptian pounds in my pocket from my friends in Jaborona, enough money for food and water on the trip. About twenty dollars, but given the sacrifices others had made to donate that money, it seemed like a fortune.

CHAPTER TWELVE

CAIRO

Here's how hundreds of thousands of Dinka refugees have traveled to Cairo: First you take a train from Khartoum north to another Sudanese city, Wadi Halfa, about a-day-and-half trip. At Wadi Halfa you change for a boat that takes you up the Nile across the Egyptian border to Aswan, where you switch to a night train for Cairo, which takes another day and a half. The train and the boat were filled with Dinka like me heading for Cairo. Some take the bus from Khartoum to Wadi Halfa because it's faster. But it is also more expensive.

It was another series of firsts for me—the train and then a boat and then another train into a new country, a new city. But my anxiety accompanied me to Wadi Halfa. I had heard too many stories about people getting stuck there. The boat they were booked on to cross the Egyptian border was not ready, or had broken down—and, with no place to stay in Wadi Halfa and no money to spare, they had to return to Khartoum. When the train arrived in Wadi Halfa, I got off and followed the crowd to a place where Sudanese officials checked our papers. My boat up the Nile would be leaving the next morning from the dock, about a fifteen-minute walk from the train. I had heard that there were places to stay for people like me without much money, and I had packed a sheet that would keep me warm. I followed others who seemed to know where these sleeping places were. They were nothing more than covered shelters where you could sleep on the ground. Families put their own rugs down, and people from the boat invited me to share their space. I lay in the dark wrapped in my sheet against the warm air, listening to voices speaking Arabic and Dinka, hoping that I would not get stuck in Wadi Halfa.

The next day the boat was at the dock, a big ferry boat, all three levels of it filled with people and cars. I showed my ticket along with my passport and visa, and I worried. "Would they let me on the boat?" The officials stared at my papers and then at me, as I listened to my heart beat faster and faster.

They waved me aboard. My papers from the black market had worked. As the boat chugged up the Nile, I went over to the snack bar and bought myself a falafel sandwich. I talked to some of the people about nothing much—where they were coming from, where they were going. Most were heading to Cairo, though some were traveling just to Aswan or all the way to Alexandria. It would be a long boat trip. I had conversations in Arabic and in Dinka.

The boat traveled up the Nile, a huge river splitting the desert, sand for as far as I could see to the east and the west. The sun moved higher in the sky and then began to come down again. Suddenly people stirred on the boat; some ran to the side to look into the river. I joined them, and there on the Nile I saw several small boats speeding toward us, five or six of them—I was too excited at the time to count—flying what people said was the Egyptian flag. Our boat slowed down and stopped, allowing the Egyptians to board. "A security check," some people said. Passengers were ordered to line up without bags, which we put through a special machine that I had never seen before. The Egyptians went through many bags and checked our papers.

But the people were happy. It meant, someone explained to me, that we had crossed the border from Sudan and entered Egyptian territory.

"Thank God, we're out of Sudan," someone said. Others said the same thing, and then I said it, "Thank God, I am finally out of Sudan."

I was happy. I celebrated with another sandwich, a shwarmaj; grilled meat in pita bread had never tasted so good as it did here in Egypt. I was enjoying my first big boat ride.

The relief of leaving Sudan and the excitement of moving to a new country blotted out for me most of the details of the trip. I remember hundreds of Dinka people, all of them as relieved as I was. We no longer had to fear a government that killed our people and destroyed our villages. When we docked at Aswan and I left the ship to connect to the night train to Cairo, I stood on Egyptian ground. My relief was complete, and I allowed myself to show the excitement I felt.

I had made it. I had no idea what was in my future, but I knew that Sudan was in my past. And that was a new feeling. (I now recognize it as the feeling of freedom.) Four hours later, I showed my ticket and papers again and climbed aboard the train to Cairo. It had been a long day of travel filled with anxiety and pleasure. I remember being tired; I don't remember falling asleep.

And then I was in Cairo. It was crazy. After almost a year in Khartoum, I thought I knew what city life was like. But Cairo is the city of cities–buildings as far as you can see, high and low, people everywhere, all the time. Khartoum has a population of five million. There are more than sixteen million people in Cairo! Of course, I had no idea of those numbers when I arrived in the Cairo train station. All I saw were people, hundreds and hundreds of people, everyone going and coming, not looking at anything, just moving quickly, so busy. I had never seen so many people so busy.

There were also many black faces, friends and family of my fellow travelers, newly arrived from Sudan. I heard the shouts of recognition, Dinka names echoing through the station. I watched men and women embrace each other, kids run into adults' arms, I saw people laugh and even cry with joy.

No one was waiting for me. Among all the millions of people in Cairo I knew not one single soul. But I had made some friends among my traveling companions, and their friends and family at the station told me that there was a place for people like me to go. If you had no one meeting you, or no address to go to, if you did not have a clue about what to do next, you could go to this church, a famous place among the south Sudanese of Cairo. A Dinka man led me there.

Sacred Heart Church was a large old building in the Sakakiny section of Cairo, a Catholic church. At 71 Hamid Street. I will never forget that address. Dinka immigrants referred to "Sacred-Heart-Church-71-Hamid-Street," as if it were one word. Everyone knew about this church. Attached to the place of worship was another structure with a large room that had been turned into a dormitory. Families were camping there within the red lines on the floor, which I realized was a basketball court. (I had seen people playing basketball in Jabarona.) Children were running around, mothers tidying up—about fifty people. Every Friday, when the train arrived in Cairo from Aswan, more people arrived. Sacred Heart also ran a school for Sudanese boys. The pastor was a priest from another country I had never heard of, "Italy."

The workers at the church, both black and white, gave me a blanket and a place to sleep on the floor. There were regular meals, and bathrooms with showers that we were allowed to use. After the chaos and noise of the refugee camp, Sacred Heart was surprisingly quiet. The people were conscious that they were living in a church building, and mothers made sure their children did not make too much noise. I didn't care. I was among my own people again. Most important of all, I was out of Sudan. For the first time since I left my mother for the marketplace in Nyamlell, I was not living under the daily threat of injury or death.

I was a free man. In Cairo.

When I was a little boy, I loved hearing of the places my father had visited: Juba, Nairobi, Uganda. I had dreamed that I, too, would travel to these places with beautiful names. Now here I was in Cairo—Egypt!—a place my own father had never been. But freedom in Cairo also meant that you had to find a place to live and some way to earn money for rent. There were no refugee camps. I knew I would not be allowed to stay at the church forever. The church was for families with no place to go. Single men like me, I was told, should be able to find places to stay. But I didn't know anyone! They shrugged, as if that was not important. Guys were kicked out every week to make room for new families.

Once again, I was faced with the question that seemed to rule my life recently: What should I do next?

I put off finding an answer for a while, enjoying the safety and regular meals at Sacred Heart. I stayed close to the church, not daring to explore the neighborhood or any other part of Cairo.

I had been among my people long enough to know how many had been killed and lost. My own life had been difficult, but I now realized how blessed I had been. I had escaped from Giemma and the police. God had kept me alive; He had provided me with Abdah, the kind Muslim truck driver who had bought me a ticket to Khartoum. And when I was sitting in the bus station in tears, alone and miserable, wondering what to do, a Dinka man appeared to help me. What my parents had told me was true: You are never alone. God is always with you. In the camp, God provided me with Garang and his family. Yes, someone had turned me into the secret police, and yes, I had been in jail for seven months. But if I hadn't been submitted to that horrible experience, I might have been satisfied to hang around Jabarona, spending my days talking to people about the awful things that happened to us, persuading myself that I was hard at work trying to find my parents. Instead, prison filled my mind with the need to leave Sudan. Within months of my release, I was on a boat across the border into Egypt.

And here I was living in a church! Shortly after my arrival at Sacred Heart I ventured inside the chapel and sat through a service. The sounds and smells sent me back to the Catholic church that my family had taken me to in Nyamlell. Sacred Heart was much bigger than the place where my family worshiped, but there was the familiar altar and statues. I smelled burning candles, incense, a mixture of perfume and sweat. I felt safe. Inside the church it was cool and quiet.

The Christians say, "May God be with you," and I had much evidence that God was at my side. I asked God for help in finding my parents, I asked Him for a better life. I still didn't know where I would live in Cairo or how, but I decided to wait for God to send me help.

He came into the hall a few days after my arrival. He was about the same height as I was. But I was skinny, and he was a big and powerful man. He walked right up to me, as if he knew who I was, and introduced himself.

"They call me Pyo," he said. His Dinka name was Tem Kuag, and he, too, was from the Aweil area. He had been a leader there, he said, a chief of a town—what we call "sultan"—who had also gone to Khartoum to be in the government. He explained that he came often to the church to pray and to check on whether any of the new arrivals were from Aweil. He had heard about me from other Dinka at the church.

"You come stay with me," he said.

I followed him outside and to his apartment building in the Abbassiya district, an easy walk from the church. Pyo and his wife had a four-bedroom apartment. They also had thirteen children living with them, including several from Pyo's other wives. He explained that he had recently been accepted by the UN as an official refugee and was getting money every month until he went to America, which, he said, would be soon. The UN money—one hundred and fifty Egyptian pounds (about fifty dollars) a month for an individual or head of family, plus

50 pounds for each dependent—could never cover the rent on such a large apartment, never mind feed and clothe Pyo's forest of Dinka boys and girls of various ages, from little ones to twenty-somethings. I learned later that, because Pyo had been such an important political figure in Aweil and was so involved in helping refugees from our area, he got "support" and "gifts" from other Dinka in Cairo, who still called him "Sultan." Unlike most people who looked out for only themselves and their families, Sultan Pyo was always helping others.

I told him my story, and, like Garang, he was not surprised. "I know about this," he said. As a chief in the south, a politician in Khartoum, and a political refugee himself, Pyo was well aware of the murahaliin attacks on our villages. Slavery, he told me, was something that existed in Sudan for centuries. While the government and many successful Sudanese denied its existence, to all Dinka slavery was part of their relationship with the Arab north, an historical fact, older than Islam itself.

"You must apply for UN refugee status," said Pyo. "Your story will help you get accepted quickly." Every Dinka in Cairo had a tragic story to tell, Pyo explained. But their stories were the same: my village was destroyed, my cattle stolen, my family was murdered, my children kidnapped, I fled to the camps in Khartoum or Kenya, I took the boat up the Nile to Aswan, the night train to Cairo—UN workers had heard it all.

"Our tragedies have become normal," said Pyo. So many people were now in Cairo trying to become official UN refugees that it had become difficult for UN officials to choose between one victim and another. The story of an escaped slave, Pyo assured me, would catch the attention of the UN refugee workers. Slavery was not yet "normal." Pyo insisted that I must apply for refugee status.

I had no idea what to do. What was this "apply"?

And that is when I learned that in Cairo, too, there was another "process"—becoming a UN-sanctioned refugee. It was what everyone talked about: who had been accepted, who was rejected, who had moved to America, Canada, England, or Australia and was sending money back to friends and family. People who had been accepted displayed their UN cards with great pride. It was an extraordinary prize. This simple piece of paper was worth 150 Egyptian pounds a month, enough to cover a single man's share of the rent and food. That card also opened up the rest of the world to you, a world of riches beyond what the refugees stuck in Jabarona could imagine. The success stories people heard from America and Europe told of jobs that paid the equivalent of thousands of Egyptian pounds a month; Dinka people even owned cars!

Pyo had already been accepted to go to America. He had helped many other Dinka with the process, and he would help me. "Your story will move them," he said. Pyo explained that the first step in the refugee process was to go to the UN offices and pick up the application for refugee status and fill it out. They wanted to know your story, and you had to tell it as strongly and accurately as possible. But first I had to get it down on paper. In English.

I could not write Arabic, never mind English.

"The English teacher will help you," he said.

. . .

"Tell me your story," said the man Pyo called "the English teacher." His name was Franco Majok, another Dinka from the province of Aweil, a man in his thirties, also with a large family. He was friendly, not as tall as I was, but a lot smarter. Franco had come to Egypt years before as a student. Back then, according to Franco, the Egyptian government had been eager to befriend the Sudanese of the south. The Nile ran through the lands of the Dinka, and Egypt needed the Nile. As a token of friendship, the Egyptian government gave scholarships to bright Dinka boys like Franco, who eventually decided to study English in Cairo. In the mid-1980s, when people began fleeing north from the civil war some headed to Cairo, because they already had relatives there who were students. Those early few turned into hundreds of thousands.

Pyo had made arrangements for someone to accompany me to the UN offices to get the application for refugee status, and now Franco would help me fill it out for the interview that had been scheduled months away, in September. These two men turned my life into a true miracle. Like Pyo, Franco had been through the UN process himself and had already earned his UN refugee status. He, too, was waiting for a date to leave for America.

I told him my story, beginning with that day my mother sent me to the marketplace, the happiest day of my life, which turned into the worst. Franco listened and wrote down what I said. Then he read it to me, and we worked on it and got it all straight: the raid, Giemma, the kids with sticks who sang the abeed song and beat me, my ten years with Giemma, and my escape to Khartoum, the secret police, my imprisonment.

Franco explained that there were many different questions

on the UN form: What happened to you? Why did you come here? What do you want us to do? All of them could be answered with various segments of my story. The UN people would read my answers and then interview me, asking questions based on what we put on the form.

"You must tell your story clearly and well," Franco explained, warning me that if any of my answers in the interview did not match what was on the form, or contradicted what we had written, I would be rejected.

"If you mess up," Franco warned. "That's it for you."

"Rejected" is the worst word a Dinka can hear in Cairo.

Franco looked at me, into my eyes. "This is your true story, Francis. This was the way it all happened."

I stared back at this man I barely knew, this "English teacher," who was now testing me for truth, and told him that no one could ever get me confused about this story. It was not only all true, it was my life.

"Everything I am telling you I saw and went through," I said. "It all happened to me. This is not something that I heard from other people. I am telling this to you from my heart."

Franco told me that I would be accepted as a refugee. "This story is very strong," he said. He had helped many people fill out their forms, but mine was the worst story he had heard—and thus the best for getting chosen as a UN refugee. Franco filled out the UN form, answering the questions according to the facts of my story.

I spent the next several months going over my story, practicing it, saying it out loud, making sure I did not miss any detail that I had reported to Franco. I even practiced it with Franco, and then I took it home and worked on it with Pyo and members of his family.

But I was never worried. "If you put everything I said on this form," I told Franco, "I will never get it wrong or forget it, because this is my life."

All I could do now was wait for my interview. During the day, Pyo's apartment was always filled with people, his kids and other Dinka looking for help, and I began exploring the nearby neighborhoods of Cairo. The sidewalks were always crowded, so many people, so busy going places, working, shopping, hanging out. Sometimes I got strange looks. "Hunga bunga!" they shouted at me, and I asked my Dinka friends what that meant. "Hunga bunga" was a phrase they used for black people, I learned. No one was sure what it meant—except trouble. "Ignore them and just keep walking," my friends advised. And I did. I never had any problems with Egyptians. I had heard about Dinka people who had been having a warm conversation with a Cairene on the street. "What religion are you?" the Egyptian would ask, and when the Dinka answered "Christian," the Muslim stepped backwards as if the Dinka had suddenly confessed to having an infectious disease. But that never happened to me. The Egyptians I met always treated me fairly. Cairo was a city of millions of people of all colors from all over the world. Unlike Khartoum, we Dinka could talk about the politics of our country without getting arrested.

The streets were clogged with cars and trucks, smoke pouring from their behinds. I was amazed at the number of shops. People were actually lined up in front of some places waiting to go in. And so many buildings—some of them rising into the sky! The Nile splits the city, and along the river are big hotels—towers of glass with green gardens filled with flowers and palm trees and swimming pools. The only Europeans I had ever seen before had been UN and Red Cross workers visiting the camps in Khartoum. In Cairo I saw many Europeans and Americans walking around in their own style of clothes and talking in their own languages. The Egyptians called them *sayiheen*—"tourists," people, Pyo explained, who traveled the world just to see the sights or for relaxing. I could not believe that people would come all the way to Cairo to relax.

I liked to go into the big shopping malls and look at the new clothes that cost one hundred or two hundred Egyptian pounds, more money than I had ever held in my hands. Pyo and other friends in the Dinka community had given me a little money to replace the dirty rags I was wearing for clothes. I bought a new shirt, trousers, and underwear in one of the neighborhood's many cheap clothing stores. And while my new things were not as beautiful as what I saw in the malls, it was the first time in my life that I had new clothes to order.

I also met a couple of young Dinka who were living in an apartment in Franco's building. Whenever Pyo's place seemed about to overflow with people, I would cross the street and sleep there. But I liked being surrounded by my people, and visited them all the time. I had spent ten years by myself talking only to the goats and cows. I could not get tired of spending time with other Dinka people, and in Cairo there were thousands to meet. I went to parties where Sudanese kids played African and Western music, hip-hop, rock and roll, even American "country" music. I visited many kinds of apartments, some small and crowded, others quite fancy.

Some Dinka had been in the city for many years and had found good jobs. They rented nice apartments with satellite TV. Their sons wore beautiful running shoes from America, just like the rich Egyptian kids and the tourists I saw in the streets. All the Sudanese boys I knew were saving their money to buy those shoes, and I decided that, if I had a lot of money, the first thing I would do was buy a pair for myself.

Most of the Dinka I knew, however, did not have jobs, and there were always plenty of people around to hang out with. While it might have looked like laziness—what was my alternative?—I saw my social life as educational. I had been dragged from the Dinka culture as a little boy, and now that I was among my people again, I wanted to learn as much as possible about my culture. It was not as easy as I had thought. Many of the kids I was socializing with in Cairo had spent their whole lives as refugees. They, too, had grown up outside of the traditional ways. I quickly discovered that they were more interested in Egyptian and Western music, movies, satellite television, and soccer. I walked into a friend's apartment one day and found everyone watching a television program featuring a bunch of black men singing and dancing.

"What's this?" I asked.

"Black Entertainment Television," someone said.

"American," said someone else.

I had no idea there were black people in America until one of my friends that afternoon informed me that more than a hundred years in the past black Africans were captured and shipped to America to work in the fields. Those American slaves were the ancestors of the guys singing on the television.

America, too, had kept abeed—black slaves like me, who were now called "African-Americans." I could not get that fact out of my mind.

As the day for my interview approached, I became more and more nervous. I had heard a lot about the UN process, and, although Pyo and Franco had been accepted, I knew that many people who had told their story had been rejected. To win at this interview, I now realized that you needed more than a story, you needed luck.

I hoped that my luck would hold, that God would not forget me today. The unlucky were truly people without hope. They could not return to Sudan, where only civil war and danger awaited them. Yet they could not leave Cairo, where they were now officially "illegal" residents. Work was scarce, even for Egyptians. But there was always the rent to pay. The churches tried to help people, but their resources were stretched to the limit, and their dormitories were already overcrowded. Every Friday the night train arrived from Aswan with more people running away from hell. For thousands and thousands who had already been through so much, that UN refugee card was their only hope. Rejection drove people crazy. I heard stories of people who killed themselves, little boys who jumped off bridges into the Nile.

It was terrible. They had escaped death in their homeland, but without that UN card they were doomed to no life in Cairo. I understood such desperation. I too knew what it felt like to prefer death to the present. If Giemma had caught me that day I headed for Mutari, I was ready for death. If he didn't kill me, I would have killed myself rather than continue a life of caring for his cows. I had told myself that, and I hope I would have had the courage to act on my convictions.

September 1 finally arrived—a good day or a bad day. Good because it would give me the chance to get my card, then the money, and then the trip to those places called "America," "Canada," "Australia," "Britain"; bad because I might be rejected immediately. They could interview you and turn you down on the spot.

The UN office was packed with people, a few hundred of them (on some days, I had heard, there could be a thousand), some like me waiting for their interviews—and others who already had been through the interview and had come to check the lists to find out whether they had been accepted or rejected. There were people crying, and there were people being hugged with happiness. I was very nervous, so nervous, in fact, that I had slept very little the night before my interview.

An Egyptian girl interviewed me. I had been asked what language I wanted to be interviewed in—English, French, or Arabic. She spoke English and Arabic and maybe even French. I chose Arabic. She was young, probably in her twenties, and she had my application in front of her, which she looked at. Then she asked me the first question:

"What happened to you?"

I told her about how when I was seven I went to the marketplace in Nyamlell. She listened very carefully, occasionally checking the form. I told her how I had been enslaved, how I had to live with a family that hated me for ten years, people who beat me and forced me to take care of their animals, people who fed me garbage.

She asked me why I came to Cairo, what I wanted the UN to do for me.

"I want to be free," I told her.

She asked me what country I wanted to go to.

I told her that I didn't care. I wanted only to leave Africa, I did not want to go back to Sudan. I said, "I just want to be safe and free."

She smiled and told me to come back in two weeks—on September 15.

As I left the office I felt good about the interview. I noticed the other people waiting. No one was smiling; everyone was as nervous as I had been. I looked at the board on the wall. There were two columns with the English words "Accepted" and "Rejected." I had been there before, and someone had told me what those words meant. Under "Rejected" there were more names than under "Accepted." On what side would "Francis Bok," as I was now known to the UN, end up?

The interview seemed to go well. I had no trouble answering any of her questions. I just told her the same story I had told to Franco. My story.

CHAPTER THIRTEEN

SEPTEMBER 15, 1998

I will never forget that date. It was the day that I returned to the UN office to find out the results of my application and interview.

Again, I had trouble sleeping the night before. I left Pyo's apartment early to catch the bus for the half-hour trip to the UN offices in the Mohandisseen area of Cairo. As soon as I walked in I heard people crying. They had been rejected and now wore the faces of people who had no future. Some people were all smiles and hugs, celebrating their acceptance. Others were pushing their way through the crowd to get closer to the lists on the wall. For most of these people the trip to these UN offices to check the lists was a weekly ritual. They had no phones or permanent addresses. The only way the UN could get the news to them was the lists on the wall. Some people, I had heard, had to wait as long as a year to find out their fates. Everyone said that I was lucky that my case was moving so quickly. But I also realized that such speed might make for a quick rejection.

"This is it," I said to myself. "This is my future." As I elbowed my way through the crowd toward the wall, a man who was pushing his way in the opposite direction said to me, "What's your name?"

"Francis Bok," I said automatically, unsure why he wanted to know.

He showed me all his teeth, a big smile. "You got accepted!" he said, patting me on the shoulder, while shouting the news to the room: "He got accepted!"

It did not register.

"You're on the list," he explained. "Accepted!"

It was a shock. Was it true? Was this guy playing with me? Did he have the right name? I pushed my way toward the list to see for myself.

There it was, near the top–*Francis Bok*. I looked to make sure my name was in the right column. Yes! *"Accepted."* I looked again, afraid that maybe my name would somehow disappear. But it was still there, *Francis Bok*.

Meantime, my messenger was telling everyone I had been accepted. People began hugging me, Dinka people I didn't even know.

"Congratulations!"

"You're very lucky!"

"This is great!"

"You're not going to Sudan anymore!"

I was filled with emotions. I stood there hugging people and accepting their congratulations. I smiled for so long that my mouth began hurting. I went to one of the officials and told them my name had appeared on the "Accepted" list. She checked my file, confirmed that I was still reachable at Pyo's number, and said that I would be contacted soon to come in and pick up my UN refugee ID card.

On the bus ride back into the city I lost track of the time. All I could think was, "I am accepted." My troubles were over. Soon I would have my ID card and be able to get my payment of 150 Egyptian pounds. I was an official UN refugee and would be leaving Cairo. Where would I go?

It did not matter to me, so long as the move improved my life. I would worry about my future later. My present was too much fun. I felt so good; I was floating through the streets. I headed immediately back to Pyo's place and ran into some of his family on the street.

"I am accepted!" I shouted. They hugged me and congratulated me. They, too, said I was lucky that the process had happened so quickly. They were on their way to a party for Franco. In all the excitement over my UN appointment, I had forgotten that Franco was flying to America that evening. I also remembered that another friend of mine was flying to Australia that night, and I had promised to go to his party a few blocks away. At the party, I told everyone that I, too, had been accepted. The next day I told everyone in my building. For days afterwards, wherever I went, Dinka people congratulated me. "We are so proud of you," they said, assuring me that I would not have any problem getting to America. I just kept smiling and laughing for days, the happiest boy in Cairo, enjoying the feeling of having my future solved. I wanted to celebrate, but I did not have the money to throw a party for my friends—or buy myself a pair of beautiful sneakers. I did not even have the money to celebrate with a tasty falafel pita.

A week later I got the call to pick up my ID card. I returned to the UN offices, showed my passport, which they checked against a list of names they had and a pile of cards folded in two—one of which they handed to me, which declared that Francis Bok was an official "United Nations refugee," and to prove it there was Francis Bok, wearing that tie they had clipped to my collar in the Dar-es-Salaam refugee camp, smiling out at me. I smiled back. I walked away staring at my ID card.

It was the most beautiful thing I had seen in Cairo.

Katusk—another famous site in Dinka Cairo is about a fifteen-minute subway ride from Pyo's. I have no idea what Katusk means in Arabic, but for the Dinka of Cairo, Katusk meant "money." The UN agency where we official refugees got our monthly payment from was in Katusk.

With my ID card safe in my pocket, I registered in Katusk, and by the end of November I received my first payment—150 Egyptian pounds. It was the most money that I had ever handled. I felt rich, but my giddiness over this extraordinary change in my life was quickly replaced by a sense of responsibility to the people who had helped me. I began contributing my share of the rent to Pyo. I gave some money to people when they needed it—just as they had given it to me. But I could not resist buying some new shirts and pants. I even bought some inexpensive sneakers. I have no idea what the rest of Cairo thought of me—six feet six inches of American-style clothes with a pair of white knockoff Nikes—but I was certain that I was looking as fine as I felt. I was sure I was looking "cool," as the hip-hop black guys said on TV.

For two Egyptian pounds I also bought my first wallet.

And then I waited. The lives of the Dinka people in Cairo are all about waiting: waiting to get an interview, waiting to get accepted, waiting for your appeal if you've been rejected, waiting for your ID card, waiting for your money, waiting to leave Cairo. There are very few jobs available and a lot of time.

But the waiting was easier with my ID in my pocket and some money in my wallet. I wandered around Cairo. (With my official refugee card, I was no longer afraid that the Egyptian police would pick me up as an "illegal resident.") I visited friends. To pass the time we played cards and watched TV. I became a soccer fan, but the game that grabbed me the most was American basketball. I loved watching those powerful, tall African-Americans speed around the court and fly through the air, flicking the ball to each other, slamming it through that hoop. It was a beautiful thing to me, and I decided that when I got to America I would start playing basketball.

I also began to take English lessons at the church. I remembered how important it was for me to learn Arabic in order to make my way in Giemma's world. I was told that in all the places that I might be sent to—the U.S., Canada, Australia, or England—the main language was English. I began learning my ABCs. The church had a free class in reading and writing English, and I enrolled. I had always been proud of how quickly I learned Arabic. But English seemed impossible. I was making little progress; I was frustrated at my inability to read the most simple things. As the prospect of moving to an English-speaking country became more real to me, I got more and more worried about the next stage of my life. Yes, I had learned Arabic, but I had spent ten years at it. How would I learn enough of this English to manage in my new country?

I also had something else to worry about: the INS. In order for me to go to America, I had to wait for the U.S. Immigration

and Naturalization Service to review my application. I had
heard that the INS rejected UN refugees all the time. There
would be another interview.

In June 1999 I returned to the UN office where I was interviewed by an INS official, an American man speaking English.
I was terrified. Friends of mine who had been through this part
of the process had warned me that it was like being in court.
Of course, I had never been in court, but they explained that
it was serious stuff, the interviewer would ask me a lot of questions, that I had to be very clear with my answers and above
all respectful.

"You must make eye contact," several people explained.
Once again, I was warned not to stray from the story that I
had told on my original UN form. That would not be a problem. I had not forgotten any detail of that story. I had lived it
for ten years, and I would never forget that part of my life,
though my days with Giemma and his family already seemed
strangely distant. I still saw Giemma and his wife in my
dreams. I still thought about those boys at the watering hole. I
often wondered what happened to the kids from my village
who also had been handed over to militiamen. And every time
I met a new person from Aweil in Cairo I asked them if they
had heard anything about my parents. But then one of my
friends would come by, or we would watch basketball on TV,
as if there were no war going on in Sudan, as if the reason why
all of us Dinka people were there in Cairo did not exist.

"Back in America," the INS man said to me, "we read your
story, and you said there was this raid, and you were taken

away. Is this true?" I had never been interviewed in English before, but I had been given a translator, an Egyptian who spoke English well and translated what the INS agent said into Arabic for me.

Once again, I told my story. The man from the INS listened carefully, and then over the next thirty minutes or so asked me more questions, but not one that I could not answer easily and with great detail.

"Thank you," he said at last. He told me that the INS would make its decision quickly, and that I should check back here at the UN offices over the next few weeks for the result. And it was over. No smile from this interviewer, no encouraging words. The translator signaled me, and we both got up from our seats and left the room. He thought it went well. I was not sure.

So the waiting began again. But I did not mind. It connected me even more closely to my community in Cairo, where everyone was constantly checking on the status of "the process." They promised to call you, but I had heard too many stories about calls that were not received. Because so many people did not have telephones, refugee and INS lists were also posted in the local churches that worked with refugees. I began dividing my Thursdays between trips to Sacred Heart and the UN offices. My life was lived around Thursday. When I didn't see my name on the list at the church, I headed off to the UN to make sure that there had not been a mistake.

Then the third Thursday, before I had checked, a friend told me that he had seen my name on the list at the church. I had been accepted to go to America! I didn't believe him. I thought he was making a joke, trying to trick me to run down to the church and find only disappointment. I went directly to the UN office—and saw my name. It was true. I would be going to America.

But I did not know which city. The INS would have to find an organization to sponsor me which typically took several more months. In the meantime, I had to have a medical checkup, the first of my life. I felt good, I was strong, I was not worried about my health, and the doctor confirmed that I was in good condition. There was also a day of "orientation," where people talked about life in America and showed us a video. They told us that Americans were nice people, friendly to strangers. They told us how the government worked, that there were plenty of jobs, but that we would have to pay taxes. I understood none of this. There were all kinds of customs and rules there that were different from Africa and Egypt. So much information, so many things that were strange to me, that I did not really take all of it in. Two statements, however, stuck in my mind:

1) At night, the streets of American cities could be dangerous. People were robbed and shot. We should be careful.

2) Everyone could go to school in America. It didn't matter if you were forty years old, you could go to school.

I had survived this long by paying attention to danger. I would be careful, too, in America. But what excited me the most was hearing that I could go to school. I don't think I heard anything the man said after that. I had already lived in Sudan, north and south; I had lived in the Jabarona camp and made many friends. Cairo was no problem for me. When I got to America, I would learn how to live there, too. I was certain of that. And maybe I would be able to go to school.

June had gone. July was soon winding down, and I was still living my life around Thursday, checking the lists at the church for my traveling date and destination. This time I double-checked at the U.S. Embassy in downtown Cairo, a few blocks from the Nile and some of the big hotels. On my way to the church hall one Thursday morning I saw a guy I knew coming toward me wearing a big smile. "Manchester, New Hampshire!" he shouted, and I had no idea what this meant. His name was on the list today, he said, and he would be going to a place called "Manchester, New Hampshire." Before I could congratulate him, he slapped me on the back.

"Your name too!" he said, laughing with joy. He informed me that my name was also on the list of those going to America. I didn't believe him. He told me to go to the church and see for myself. I decided to go straight to the American Embassy. I walked into the Embassy to the area where the lists were put up, and there it was—four names down the list, "Francis Bok." Next to my name was my travel date: August 13, 1999. My sponsor would be a Christian group, Lutheran Social Services. They would help me settle in a place called "Fargo, North Dakota."

CHAPTER FOURTEEN

AMERICAN JOURNEY

TWA Flight 891, Cairo to JFK, New York, August 13, 1999; departure time: one A.M. From JFK I would then fly to Chicago, O'Hare, for a connecting flight to Fargo, North Dakota. New names on an intinerary.

I threw a party. Whenever any of us left Cairo there was a party. During a year in Cairo I had met many people, and many more I hadn't met also showed up that evening in the apartment I was sharing with two friends since Chief Pyo had left for America a few months before. The party cost me almost two hundred Egyptian pounds (about seventy dollars), a big chunk of my savings from my UN payments. It was a lot of money, but a party was expected. Many people had helped me, and I wanted to share my happiness about going to America. They began showing up in the late afternoon. The women cooked Sudanese food—chicken and beef with traditional sauces. Before long, the place was packed with people enjoying themselves almost as much as I was.

But at about nine I decided it was time for me to leave for the airport. Wearing my best clothes and the rest of what

I owned (two pairs of pants and a few shirts) packed in a
school bag, carrying my passport, my UN refugee folder, and
fifty dollars American that the UN had given me when they
closed my file, I took the bus from Abbassiya to the Cairo Airport. I was told to get to the airport at least two hours before
my one o'clock flight. I decided to get there by ten to give
myself plenty of time to check in and get through the long lines
for various security checks. The bus headed for al-Uruba, the
airport road, past the Cairo Exhibition Grounds, a huge green
park. I had been to the airport before, to say goodbye to Pyo
but I had never been inside the terminal. For security reasons,
only ticket holders were allowed inside. How I had longed to
be a ticket holder.

Now I was, and not only a ticket holder but an official trav-
eler to America, to Fargo, North Dakota. I still had no idea
where Fargo was, how big it was, what kind of people lived
there. Many refugees showed up at the airport with no idea
what country they were flying to. Every place outside of Africa
was a mystery to them. At least I knew the name of my new
country.

It was my turn to say good-bye to my closest friends who
had joined me for the bus ride to the terminal. They embraced
me, I embraced them. I wished them luck in their own "pro-
cesses." We would stay in touch. Inside the terminal I saw the
TWA counter and checked in, making my way through the
security posts to the gate where the plane would be leaving for
New York–JFK. It was hard for me to believe I was flying to
New York, a place I had heard about on Egyptian television. I
saw several black faces, including the guy who was going to
Manchester, New Hampshire, who told me that we would be

flying with five families from Somalia and Sudan, also spon-
sored by the Lutheran Social Services. We all sat together in
the terminal, a bit stunned by the scene around us. The first
thing I noticed was how mixed the crowd was. We were a
handful of Africans surrounded by hundreds of Egyptians,
other Arabs, and many white people, the sort of well-dressed
American and European tourists that I had seen on the streets
of Cairo. The other thing I noticed was how comfortable they
all seemed about traveling, how experienced they were, while
we Africans huddled together, a band of anxious refugees waiting to fly through the air into the unknown.

"What would you like to drink?" The woman working on the
plane was talking to me in English, and I had no idea what she
was saying. But she was handing out bottles of wine and cups
of coffee and tea to other people.

"Tea," I said. She smiled and handed me a cup of tea, which
I tasted. No sugar. I liked lots of sugar in my tea, but I did not
know how to ask for more. I did not even have the courage to
ask the other Sudanese on the plane to help me. Surely they
would think I was stupid not to know how to get sugar for my
tea. When she returned to clean up I gave her back my full cup
of tea, worried that she would be annoyed. But she smiled at
me and took away my cup without a word. Soon she was back
with a hot meal, chicken, that tasted fine. After the trays were
taken away I settled back in my seat. It was now the middle of
the night, Cairo time, and all my partying, topped with the
anxiety of traveling to a strange place had finally caught up
with me. I pulled my blanket around me and looked forward

to some sleep. But something strange was happening to my ears. They kept getting blocked up. I would slap them with my hands, which seemed to help for a while, until they got stopped up again as if they had suddenly filled with water. I fell asleep, woke up again, and nodded off once more.

The plane arrived at JFK at six A.M., local time, and everyone clapped. I didn't. I wasn't quite sure why they were clapping, and I was not used to clapping for anything. For some reason the sound of clapping embarrassed me.

But I was excited to be on the ground. In America! From the window I could see lines of big jets with TWA and other names marked on them. I grabbed my bag, made sure I had my ticket and my documents, and joined the passengers leaving the plane. The Somalians, the Sudanese, and I followed the crowd through a series of corridors to a roomful of people standing in queues. Everyone was speaking English and I didn't understand a word. One man came up to me and said something. I had no idea what he wanted. He began talking again, and I just stood there, and then I heard a familiar word—"passport." I gave my passport to him, and he went over to a nearby office. Before I could get too worried that I would never see him again, he returned to show me that my passport had been stamped. He also handed me a card—the I-94, which grants you temporary entry into the United States until you receive your "green card," allowing you to work in the U.S. without being an American citizen.

That was it. I took one more look at the stamp on my passport—and also saw the picture of Francis Bok smiling. I smiled back. I was officially inside America. And if I doubted the fact, all the English I was hearing proved it: lots of English, sound after sound with no meaning. Suddenly I was worried again: How was I going to communicate with these Americans? They spoke so quickly. I saw the other refugees from the plane moving and I followed them. We were being hustled out to make our connections. The TWA terminal at JFK was a beautiful place, with more glass and steel and carpets than the Cairo airport, much more beautiful. Even though it was so early in the morning, the airport seemed crowded with people hurrying someplace. As we were shown the way to our different gates, I marveled at the shops and the food places. I wanted to look more closely, but we didn't have time. I said good-bye to the Sudanese going to New Hampshire and followed the people going to Chicago–O'Hare.

At O'Hare we were on our own, with some time before our flight to Fargo, and I got to see the shops and the food court. So many things to buy, to eat, though none of the food was familiar to me and therefore not at all appetizing. The airport itself was gigantic, the biggest indoor place I had every seen, filled with well-dressed people hurrying one way and the other, seeming to know exactly where they were going.

We were not so sure. I was now with another Dinka and his wife who were also going to Fargo, plus a Somalian woman with many bags who would be going on from Fargo to Minnesota. The TWA people had told us to go to "F-3." There was A and B, C and D, E, and finally F–"Terminal F." But there were so many Fs, and my ability to read the American numbers was limited. Where was this F-3? We were looking for F-3, and everyone was looking at us–these very tall Africans in their strange clothes among thousands of American businessmen with their ties and sleek suits, their shiny shoes and bags, charging every which way—into the As, Bs, Cs, the Ds, Es, Fs. (Learning my ABCs at Sacred Heart Church in Cairo had some use after all.)

We were lost. We approached a group of people near the food court and asked where F-3 was and they pointed us the way. We followed their directions, but no F-3. A big black man in a uniform putting garbage bags into a push cart noticed our confusion and joined us. He said something that none of us understood. "F-3," I said, waving my ticket. "F-3." He checked my ticket and led us down the corridor a ways, stopped, and pointed down another big corridor.

"F-3," he said and smiled. We nodded, smiled back, headed in that direction—and there it was: the sign for F-3. Relieved to get there, I now had time to realize that the first person to help me in America was a black man. I had seen these black Americans on TV in Cairo, people who had originally been shipped from Africa as slaves, and were now free people, African-Americans like this friendly man working at Chicago–O'Hare. And here I was also in O'Hare Airport, an African in America.

The plane landed in Fargo when the sun was low in the sky, about 5 P.M. I had been traveling for more than twenty-four hours and my body was not sure whether it was day or night. My head felt as if it was filled with sand.

As I exited the plane I was greeted by an African who worked for Lutheran Services, a Somalian named Ahmed.

"Welcome to America!" he said with a big smile. Although I did not understand much of what he said, I made out the word "apartment." He helped the Sudanese couple with their bags and gestured for us to follow him. He kept talking, but I did not mind not understanding. Here in this strange new place I was happy to have someone taking charge. We followed him to his vehicle, which looked to me like an army truck (I now know it was an SUV), threw our bags in the back, and climbed inside. We then rode into town, where he dropped off the couple at an apartment building. I waited inside the car while he brought their stuff inside, wondering where I would be living.

Ahmed took me to another apartment building about twenty minutes away on the other side of town, a nice, clean building, newer than the ones I had known in Cairo. I followed him to a door on the ground floor that he unlocked. He told me to go in. There was a living room, a kitchen, a bathroom, a bedroom. He opened the cupboards to show me dishes and food in boxes and cans; he opened the refrigerator, which was filled with milk, eggs, and more food. He explained that this beautiful apartment was mine.

Before I could figure out what to say he had handed me the key and was out the door. I sat down on the sofa and looked around. I realized that I was smiling. "Is this real?" I thought. "Am I really out of Sudan, out of Egypt, out of Africa, and here in America?" I looked around at the furniture, the little TV; I pounded the cushion of my sofa. Yes, it was all real. I was actually sitting in my own apartment in America.

I was hungry. I returned to the kitchen and reexamined some of the boxes and cans that Ahmed had shown me. The pictures were unfamiliar, and I could not read the labels or the directions. I had learned to cook on my own in Cairo on an electric stove not much different from the one in the apartment.

But I was afraid that if I mixed foods I did not know, I might get sick, maybe even poison myself. I went to the refrigerator and pulled out a carton of orange juice—I could tell from the pictures of oranges on the box—and drank it.

I turned on the TV set and sat down on the sofa to watch. The picture was not clear, the sound was strange and noisy, on all the channels. As I stared at the bad picture in my apartment in Fargo, North Dakota, U.S.A., my mind suddenly traveled back to northern Sudan, to Giemma's farm, to those days when I did not dare do the things I wanted to do. Then I was at the watering place where I first saw the other Dinka boys, the kids who had not escaped. My own freedom emphasized their slavery. I found myself thinking about all those days—years really—when my head was full of dreams of escaping, when I would pass the time making getaway plans. And for the first time, I began to wonder how I might help those Dinka slaves get away from the river and the cows and the masters who beat them and cut off their legs. I began to wonder about the good things I might do now that I was free—how I might be able to rescue them from northern Sudan and get them into a nice apartment like the one I was sitting in. I wanted them to be free like me. I knew how they felt; I wanted them to know how I felt, now that I was on my own, in this place called "Fargo."

The fatigue finally hit me. I was exhausted by my trip across so many different worlds and time zones. I took a shower, enjoying the silence of my own bathroom—in Cairo we all had to share a shower—and then climbed into my new bed, the softest bed I had ever felt. As I lay there in the dark trying to empty my mind to make room for sleep, I began thinking about the kids from Gourion who went with me to the marketplace.

What had happened to Kvol? Was he, too, still tending a mura-haliin's cattle? What about Nyabol and Abuk? The girls my mother put in charge of me would be women now. Were they working for Arab families, maybe not so far away fom Giemma's place? I hoped they had not been hurt; I hoped that they, too, had escaped and returned to their parents.

But I had no idea what happened to those friends from my village. I still don't.

CHAPTER FIFTEEN

STILL "A GOOD WORKER"— BUT NOW A PAID ONE

I used to stand in the Fargo apartment and just stare at the kitchen—*my* kitchen, filled with my pots and my pans, my plates and my glasses. I could use all of this any time I wanted to. I could go outside, look around, then come back, unlock the door, and go anywhere in that apartment I wanted to. Into the bathroom to wash up, into the bedroom to lie down to take a nap, then back into the kitchen for a little something to eat— whatever I wanted. I could even take my food into the living room where I could sit down and turn on my little TV by remote control.

"I can do anything I want here," I used to say to myself as I walked around the apartment, so clean and newly painted, plain but pretty to my eye. I had a bathtub and a shower all to myself.

No one could tell me, "Do this!" and "Do that!"

One day I'm in Cairo, anxious about my first plane trip to America, and the next I'm lying on a bed in my own apartment in Fargo, North Dakota. This was amazing to me. A miracle! It was perfect.

Except for the bed. It was clean and comfortable, to be sure, a brand new bed with nice white sheets and a warm blanket from the local Wal-Mart. But this bed was much too short for me. This was a bed made for Americans and not for six-foot-six-inch-tall Dinka refugees.

The TV was also a problem. The reception was not good and the channels were few. But then again, I didn't understand what they were saying on the TV anyway.

Within a few days I was cooking for myself. That first morning after arriving from Egypt I woke up hungry. I investigated the cans again. From the pictures I figured out some were filled with soup, others with some kind of fruit I did not recognize. But I was still afraid to eat unfamiliar food. I drank more juice. Fortunately, Ahmed came by to check on me and noticed I hadn't eaten anything.

"I'll be right back," he said. About a half hour later he returned with a large flat box—my first pizza. Ahmed opened the box to reveal the contents, as if it were a gift. But I did not like Ahmed's present. It did not look like good food to me; it seemed messy. And though I didn't say it to Ahmed, who seemed very proud of his pizza, this "pizza" thing looked very much like garbage to me. I refused to eat it.

"I'll be right back," said Ahmed once again, and he soon returned with a bag full of beef and chicken wings. This was familiar food that I knew how to cook—and I did. The first big meal I made for myself was a feast of eggs and beef boiled Sudanese-style with onions. Very tasty.

I spent the next several weeks settling into my new life in Fargo. I began exploring the food in the apartment, figuring out what was in the cans and boxes from the pictures on the sides. Ahmed helped me read the directions, and when I ran out of food he bought me more, and so did Latetia, an ex-refugee from Liberia who became my "caseworker" from the Lutheran Services and checked up on me almost every day. I soon figured out where the nearest stores were and began buying my own food with the money that the Lutherans were giving me. They had also given me a bicycle for getting around town, and it must've been a comical sight for the locals to see this tall, skinny African pedaling down the street not entirely in control of his two-wheeled vehicle. I had learned to ride a bicycle in Egypt, but not expertly. People stared at me as if they had never seen anything like a Dinka built like a pole. One person said, "I've seen other people like you," referring to the other Dinka in the Fargo area. They seemed nice, these citizens of Fargo, and no one yelled out "hunga bunga," as the people of Cairo did when we passed. Yet, looking back on my life in Fargo, I remained quite cautious during my entire stay. I was reluctant to stray too far from my own neighborhood to explore the city. Once I discovered the wonders of the local Wal-Mart, I had no reason to shop anyplace else; Wal-Mart (there was a K-Mart, too) already had aisles and aisles of things I did not need.

I had this new life, but I was still not comfortable in it. Fargo was like a pair of shoes that needed some wearing. I was still thinking ahead too much, anticipating threats to my sense of self and well-being. What if I got lost? My English was nonexistent. And there was that comment the man made at the "orientation" in Cairo—that America could be dangerous at night, when people got shot on the streets. As eager as I was to enjoy my new freedom, embarrassment and danger fenced me in.

I did not like the weather, either. August was very hot in Fargo. I had spent my childhood standing around in watering places in sun that could boil men's blood; the summer heat in Cairo could register more than one hundred degrees for weeks, and I managed. But in Fargo's heat the sweat poured off my body.

"It's the humidity," Ahmed said. He had lived in Fargo for years and tried to explain the difference between the dry desert heat I was used to Africa and this soggy American variety.

"Wait a few months," he said. "It will be really tough for you."

This worried me. Things were now so good. I did not need any more "tough" in my life. "What will happen to me?"

Ahmed laughed. "It will be really cold come November and December," he explained. "Lots of snow. You are now living in one of the worst places in America for snow."

I shrugged. After what I had been through, how bad could it be?

"We've got a job for you!" Latetia announced over the phone. I rushed over to the Lutheran Social Services office, where Leticia introduced me to one of her coworkers, a Kurd from Iraq who spoke Arabic. He had found me a job—eight hours a day, 3 P.M. to 11 P.M., five days a week, at seven dollars an hour.

"It's the only job available," he explained. The company was located within a decent bicycle's ride from my apartment, and it didn't matter whether I spoke English. "They make pallets." I had no idea what a pallet was.

The next day I was a pallet maker. Latetia and the Kurd drove me to the place and introduced me to my employers. I was handed a pair of goggles to protect my eyes, and a cover for my nose and mouth, and led into the workshop. I had seen these wooden things before in Sudan and Egypt, used for storing and loading. My job was to build new pallets, often using dirty wood from old ones that were beyond repair. The boss showed me the routine: I had to go over to where the wood or old pallets were and carry as much as I could across the shop to a big table where we set the wood in place and nailed the new pallets together with a nail gun. I would then lift the finished pallet off the worktable and stack it on a pile of other new pallets, which another worker would take away in piles of twenty with a forklift. I would then head off to get more material and lug it back to the worktable.

That was my job, all day and every day. At the end of the week I got my first salary check—for $280, minus taxes. "In America, everyone pays taxes to the government," Latetia explained. I was taking home $240. And that's what I did, take it home. Excited as I was to hold in my hand the first money I had ever been paid for my work, I had no idea how to turn my first paycheck into real money. I kept that first check for several days, until Latetia came to my rescue and helped me open a bank account. I quickly realized that in a month I would have almost a thousand dollars, a fortune in Cairo. My rent, which Lutheran Services had been paying, was under two hundred a month. In my mind, I could see the money piling up over the next several months, thousands of green dollars piled higher than a stack of pallets.

Unfortunately, I doubted that I could do this job for

another week, never mind for several months. It was a terrible job, dirty and dangerous. If four or five people were working the saws, we would disappear in the dust and dirt, which was no match for the nose and mouth guard. Within a few minutes on the job all you could smell and taste were wooden pallets. Other workers sometimes walked right into me because they didn't see me—and I didn't see them. Little pieces of wood bounced off my clothes and goggles. More worrisome were the nails. We used nail guns, and it wasn't unusual for a stray nail to whiz past like a bullet. By the time I rode my bicycle through the empty streets of Fargo to get back to my apartment just before midnight, my muscles were aching from all that pallet carrying. My clothes were filthy, and my body was covered with sweat and dirt. It took me as long as thirty minutes in the shower to scrub the pallet-making off me.

For ten years I had been forced to work with Giemma's animals, but not once had I returned home as weary and dirty as I was every night after a shift in the pallet shop.

I lasted two weeks at the pallet company—long enough to know I hated the job and to be able to say so in English. But I did not tell Latetia or anyone else at the agency. It was their responsibility to set me up in Fargo and find me a job. After that, I was on my own. After all, I was now a free man, and I decided that my first act of freedom in America would be to quit my job.

The Great Plains Plastic Company. I will never forget that name or my work there churning out knobs for "stick shifts," as I quickly learned the gear shifts for standard transmission

cars were called. I met a Sudanese guy who had also been settled in the Fargo area with his wife. Because of a slight disabil-
ity, he was not fit for working in the pallet company and had
to look for another job in town. He told me I should go to the
Great Plains Plastics Company.

Great Plains Plastics was about a fifteen-minute walk from
where I lived. Again, I was working the late shift, this time four
to midnight. But the work was a lot easier, cleaner, and my
supervisor, Mohammed, another Kurd from Iraq, spoke Arabic. Mohammed took me to a machine and showed me what I
had to do: Sitting in a chair close to this big machine, you took
a sheet of plastic material, placed it in one end of the machine
and waited until it came out the other end of the machine as a
bunch of gear shift knobs. Any still stuck to the original material you had to cut off with a pair of scissors. The finished
knobs went into a big box.

Simple. But still dangerous. The material routinely got
stuck in the machine. The first time it happened, I tried to pick
it out—and almost lost my hand. Mohammed warned me to
stop the machine before I tried to clear it, and I took his advice.
I had managed to keep all my body parts during ten years in
northern Sudan, and I was not about to lose one to an American machine.

The pay, too, was good. Amazingly, after only two weeks in
the American workforce, I received a forty-dollar-a-week raise.
Great Plains Plastics was paying me eight dollars an hour.

"You have to work hard," Mohammed warned me. "That's
how they do it here in America. People who had your job got
fired because they didn't do it well. So when the manager is
here, you better work hard."

The boss, an American whose name I cannot remember, was, as Americans seemed to say all the time, "a nice guy." He actually stopped at my machine a few times to say, "You're a good worker. Really good." I didn't spend a lot of time talking to the other guys or extending my coffee break, as some of the others liked to do. I was often the last to turn off my machine when it was coffee-break time, and I often returned to work a couple of minutes before the break officially ended.

As much as I liked to work, to be honest, I was also eager to avoid talking to people. Most of my fellow twenty or so workers were Americans, and English flowed out of their mouths faster than my brain could comprehend. Whenever something went wrong, no matter how hard I tried to explain the problem, the Americans and Bosnians who worked in the factory could not understand me. My poor English thus turned into a major incentive for not messing up and working hard. There were several other Arabic speakers, four Kurds in addition to Mohammed, a Somalian who also spoke Arabic, and a few Liberians. I ended up becoming friends with a Liberian guy, in his twenties and closer to my age, who had worked at the company for seven years. He had a name that I had so much trouble pronouncing that I avoided using it and have since forgotten. He lived in my neighborhood, and occasionally stopped by my apartment after work. His English seemed pretty good, and as we talked I tried to listen to how he said things and remember the words he used. It was a method that had helped me learn Arabic, and I continued to listen hard to people speaking English at work and on television, repeating words, and talking to my Liberian friend.

. . .

Working at night turned my days upside down. When I came home after midnight I would have something to eat, watch a little TV or listen to the radio, and then go to bed. My life in Fargo took on the routine of going to work, coming home from work, and resting up for work. The weeks passed, then months, and I began to feel a kind of cold in the air that I had never felt before. As I rode my bike, I could barely hold onto the handlebars, they were so cold; the wind stung my cheeks. I bought a warm hat and a pair of gloves. In Sudan and Egypt I could not control the heat, and in Fargo the cold was also something I knew I would have to live with. At least I could afford to buy the warm clothes I needed, and my apartment was very cozy.

One day I awoke and noticed that the apartment was still dark. It was mid-morning, when the room was usually quite bright. But I couldn't even see out the window. I pulled up the blinds to see that the window seemed to be covered with something. I tried to open it, but the window was stuck.

When I walked outside, I could not believe how much white there was. It had snowed so hard since I had come home from work that the first floor of the building was almost buried in the stuff. I touched the snow. It was cold and then melted in my hand. So much snow did not seem normal to me, and I got scared. But I needed food and milk from the store. Trucks were plowing the street, creating dunes of snow on the side of the road. The sidewalk near the building was also clean. I walked out to look around—and almost fell down. The walk was shiny and my feet slipped and slid. But I could see cars on the road moving along fine. I decided to ride my bike.

A big mistake. I headed down the road, moving along quite well. But when I approached the corner and applied the brakes the wheels locked, but the bike kept moving—and fell over, pitching me into a pile of snow. One second I'm riding my bike, the next second I'm a snowman. I brushed myself off, picked up my bike and got back on, foolishly. I skidded and slid, until I realized that the next fall I took might be in front of a car. I got off the bicycle and walked it to the store, slipping and sliding on the ground with Ahmed's words echoing in my head: "You are now living in one of the worst places in America for snow."

I was lonely in Fargo. After work I watched sports on TV and listened to the radio. The parties in Cairo usually included lots of American music, rock and roll and hip-hop. I enjoyed listening to all kinds of music, and in Fargo that included country, classical, and jazz. In Cairo I had a wide circle of friends. The Dinka of Cairo had little money, but we were rich in time, and we spent it hanging out with other south Sudanese. According to Latetia and Ahmed, there were a few hundred Dinka in the area and about four thousand Nuer, the second largest tribe in southern Sudan, who, I've since discovered, account for 65 percent of the 17,000 southern Sudanese in the U.S. I was eager to meet these people and speak my language or Arabic. But I soon discovered that these other Africans lived too far from me to get to by bicycle, and Fargo's public transportation was poor. Every American seemed to own a car. Lutheran Services was helpful in trying to get people from southern Sudan together to make our transition to life in

America easier. But the ancient tensions between the Nuer and Dinka have followed us to America, making socializing difficult. I eventually met some people from the Nuba Mountains and Juba, the city in the far south of Sudan where my father used to go for business. But they were from different tribes, and we had little in common apart from our refugee status.

I had heard that there were many Dinka in Iowa, in a city called Des Moines and another place called Ames. I met a Dinka guy from Sioux Falls, South Dakota, who had lived in Fargo and was visiting friends. He, too, had lived Cairo. In fact, he was planning to move to Ames in six months to be closer to other friends from Cairo—people from Aweil whom I had also known in Cairo!

I had wondered what happened to Adel, her husband, their children and Adel's two brothers, especially Dau Dau, whose going away party I had attended in Cairo a month before I myself left. They were part of a very well-known and influential family in Aweil. I had no idea that they were so near, and I was eager to talk to Adel and Dau. The guy from Sioux Falls gave me Adel's telephone number, and I called her right away. Adel was happy to hear from me and told me that there was a big community of people from Aweil in Ames. They also mentioned some other friends of mine from Cairo who were living in Des Moines. Right then I knew I had to go to Iowa. I told Adel that, in spite of my good-paying job and nice apartment, I was not happy in Fargo.

"You're welcome here," she said. "Come and stay with us."

The next day I told the people at Lutheran Services I was leaving Fargo, that my friends in Ames had invited me to stay with them. I would find a job in Ames. Latetia and Ahmed wished me well, I thanked them for all their help, and then went to the bus station to buy my ticket. I got a reservation on the bus to Minneapolis, where I would switch to another bus that went directly to Ames. My departure date: January 1, 2000.

Everyone, of course, told me that I was crazy to travel on this big day, the beginning of "the New Millennium." Some people warned that it would be dangerous. Who knows what would happen on such an unusual day? Others said it was a day for celebration, that I would be missing the fun.

But I wanted to get to Ames. I wanted to be close to a big group of people, my people, friends from Aweil, who shared not just my language but my customs. I had spent most of my life alone, separated from my people and culture. And now that I was a free man in a free country with the price of a bus ticket in my pocket, it made no sense to me to have to sit around an apartment, no matter how nice, with no one to talk to and laugh with.

I decided that January 1, 2000, would be a new beginning for me—of my life in America among my own people.

They were waiting for me at the bus station in Ames—Adel and her brother Dau Dau. I hadn't seen them since 1998, when they left Cairo. They gave me a big hug and took me home. This was my idea of a truly happy New Year!

I moved into their big house in Ames, almost a Dinka village in itself, filled with their relatives: Adel's mother and her husband, their three children, her two brothers, three assorted uncles and cousins. Twelve people. All from the Aweil area.

Yes, I had given up my own apartment to share a room

with Dau Dau. But I loved the company. In Fargo, I didn't have anyone I could talk to regularly in my own language. Now I was with a house full of people of all ages with whom I could communicate and who could help me understand life in America better. When I said something wrong in English they would laugh at me. I didn't mind because they would then tell me how to say it correctly. They had been to school in Africa, in Egypt, and in the States. Some were even in college. Dau Dau not only could speak English quite well, he also could read and write Arabic.

I loved having so many people around. I didn't even mind when they corrected my Dinka. The musical tastes of the young people were more refined than mine, and they began introducing me to their favorite hip-hop records, which soon became my favorites, too. Then I discovered Reggae music, which is now my favorite.

Dau Dau helped get me a job at the Burke Corporation, a meatpacking company where he worked. I worked the night shift—from ten to seven—cleaning their meatpacking machines and the floors with chemicals. After a couple of weeks, I found a second job on the housekeeping staff at the local Holiday Inn for six hours a day, which I soon was able to extend to full time. I would go directly from the meatpacking plant to the motel, putting in a sixteen-hour workday. I was making $690 a week— $9.25 an hour at Burke, plus $8 an hour at the Holiday Inn.

America was generous to me. Everyone in Cairo had said that life in America was great, and so far I had not been able to prove them wrong. I liked America, and I did my best to fit in. My friends even began teasing me about being "so American-ized." I loved American clothes. I had four or five pairs of cool sneakers, hip-hop-style jeans and shirts. A shelf full of baseball caps. I liked nice clothes, and now that I had the money I could buy not just what I needed but also what I liked. If I saw a shirt or a jacket that looked good in a store, I bought it. Strangers were surprised to find out that I was such a recent arrival to America. I even bought myself a pair of wire-rimmed glasses, the kind I saw the college students wearing. I went into a store and pointed to the pair I liked. "Do you wear contacts?" the sales woman asked me. I told her my eyes were fine. "I just need them for fun." She seemed surprised that I would be willing to buy a pair of frames for more than one hundred dollars "just for fun." But I liked the way I looked in glasses. Sometimes I would buy things because it made me happy. I had known sadness and misery and real pain. I preferred being happy, and sometimes I just went out and bought some happiness.

As much as I loved being part of Adel's family, I needed to get my own place, something I could share with one of the many new friends I was meeting through Adel's ever-widening circle of Dinka in Ames and Des Moines. I also wanted to go to school. It was becoming clear to me that the Dinka people I met, who had some education, were succeeding more easily than those who stuck to the old ways. That was the one thing that really struck me about life in America: everyone was well educated. Among my people in Sudan, few had been to school. In America, I discovered that even three-year-old kids were in school. You did not need money to be able to get an education. America seemed to try to give everyone a chance. If you went to school and worked hard, you could make a wonderful life for your family. I saw it all around me, not just among the Americans, but also my Dinka friends. In Sudan and Egypt, opportunities were available only to a few. In America, the opportunities seemed limitless—for everyone, including us immigrants. In Iowa, I saw people I had known in Cairo when we were all poor. Now they had jobs, money, nice clothes, and beautiful cars. Some were already going to college in an effort to get better jobs.

"It may seem impossible to you to get where you want to get," they said to me. "But when you stay in America longer, you will see that you will be able to get the same things we have—good jobs, a nice apartment, a car—anything you want." But improving your English was crucial, they advised, as was getting as much formal education as you could. I decided that I would work hard to make enough money to be able to take some time off to go to school. There were so many things to learn about the world, and I knew so little.

I was making some progress. My English was getting good enough to make myself understood at work. On the job, I was forced to learn how to read simple instructions; with the help of friends and fellow workers, I began to decipher job applications and the other forms and documents that seemed as big a part of American life as cars and television. Even to do something as simple as taking the bus, I had to be able to read signs and posters. And, like any teenager, I was eager to learn how to drive. I disliked having to depend on someone at the house to give me a ride to work and pick me up. Adel taught me how to drive and then helped me pass my driver's test. (Immigrants with language problems are allowed to have a translator sit with them during the test.) After I got my license, she lent me one of the four cars in the family, so that I could drive to work at night and hand it over to Dau Dau, when I returned home in the morning, for his drive to the meat plant to begin his shift.

In the little spare time I had, I began playing some basketball. I had seen kids playing the game in Cairo, and I became a big Los Angeles Lakers fan in Fargo, watching games on television. The Shaquille O'Neal and Kobe Bryant Lakers were winners, and I, too, wanted to be a winner. In Ames, I actually played basketball for the first time. We lived near Iowa State University, which allowed neighborhood people to use the gym. I joined a group of Dinka who played there regularly. My enthusiasm was high; my shooting skills were low.

After two months I had enough money to rent a $420-a-month, two-bedroom apartment with my friend Aguan Aguan, another Dinka who had lived in America since 1995. Even with my rent and living expenses, I was still saving enough money to spare $350 for a friend in Cairo who had been rejected by the UN and couldn't find a job. It gave me so much pleasure to send money to someone. So many people had helped me, were still helping me in fact, that I wanted to take a turn doing some good.

Life in Ames, Iowa, was pretty sweet. After twelve years of slavery and exile, I felt that I had finally found a home.

Then, in April 2000, I got a call from this guy in Boston.

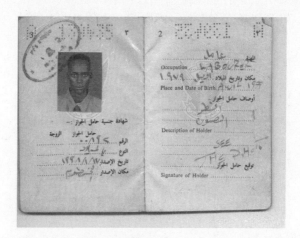

My Sudanese passport includes the first photo ever taken of me, when I was 18.

On September 18, 2000, the same afternoon that I testified to the Senate, I was invited with a group of fifth graders from the STOP Slavery campaign to meet Secretary of State Madeleine Albright. She was much shorter than me, but a very strong woman. COURTESY OF THE STATE DEPARTMENT

At the White House signing ceremony for the Sudan Peace Act, I was very happy to meet Condoleeza Rice, President Bush's National Security Advisor. COURTESY OF THE AMERICAN ANTI-SLAVERY GROUP

Juneteenth is a holiday that commemorates the day that African-American slaves in Texas first learned of the abolition of slavery. In 2001, I spoke at a Juneteenth celebration on Capitol Hill with members of Congress and the great-grandson of Frederick Douglass. COURTESY OF THE AMERICAN ANTI-SLAVERY GROUP

Without knowing it, I was nominated by a student to be a torch-bearer for the 2002 Winter Olympics. I was selected to run with the torch by Plymouth Rock. As I ran with the torch, I remembered running away from Giemma toward freedom. COURTESY OF THE AMERICAN ANTI-SLAVERY GROUP

At the 2001 Coachella Music Festival in Palm Springs, the band Jane's Addiction asked me to come on stage during the encore. Here I am with singer Perry Farrell speaking to the crowd of forty thousand. COURTESY OF THE AMERICAN ANTI-SLAVERY GROUP

One of my most important early speaking appearances was in December 2000 at Harvard's Kennedy School of Government. I was joined by Jay Williams, a Harvard student who has helped rescue thousands of slaves in Sudan; Jesse Sage, the associate director of the American Anti-Slavery Group; and Wendy Patten, from the White House. COURTESY OF THE AMERICAN ANTI-SLAVERY GROUP

Shortly after the September 11 attacks, a friend took me to visit
Ground Zero. I looked out at the rubble and realized that Osama bin
Laden had been living in Sudan while I was held in slavery. There was
an eerie connection between my enslavement and what had just happened in New York City. PHOTO BY JAMES LEVINE

At the White House signing ceremony for the Sudan Peace Act, I was
introduced to President Bush. He shook my hand, and we spoke for
several minutes about my story. I thanked him on behalf of all the children still in slavery in Sudan. PHOTO BY KEVIN LAMARQUE. REUTERS 2002.

John Eibner, who is in charge of Christian Solidarity International's slave redemption program and who helped find my brother, stands in front of a Dinka home (called a *tukul*) that had been burned and destroyed during a slave raid. COURTESY OF CHRISTIAN SOLIDARITY INTERNATIONAL

Some children bear the physical scars of slavery. This boy, Magok Fiel, was captured in a slave raid in 1995. He was shot in the upper arm, but a militia raider still bound Magok by his arm to a horse, dragging him along until his arm was severed. He was then left unconscious to die, but he was rescued after the raid. COURTESY OF CHRISTIAN SOLIDARITY INTERNATIONAL

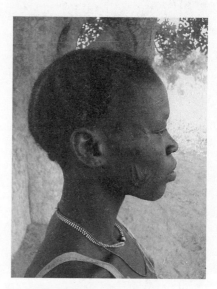

A slave owner branded this young woman on her face to mark her as his property. COURTESY OF CHRISTIAN SOLIDARITY INTERNATIONAL

Slave rescuers collect children captured in slave raids and bring them back to their villages and their families. I look into the eyes of the children waiting to be redeemed and remember the deep pain of slavery. COURTESY OF CHRISTIAN SOLIDARITY INTERNATIONAL

CHAPTER SIXTEEN

THE NEW ABOLITIONISTS

He said he worked for some kind of group that opposed slavery, and that Franco Majok had told him about me. I was still in touch with Franco, the English teacher who had filled out my UN form. Franco was now living in the Boston area, working as a caseworker for the Lutheran Social Services. He had given this American my telephone number.

When he called, however, I was at work, and my roommate Aguan Aguan had taken the message. But I was not interested in talking about slavery. I had been trying to put Sudan behind me and find a new life here in Iowa. In a strange way, I was trying to find the life I had lost in Ames. I was a Dinka man, unmistakably so here in the Midwest of America. ("I've seen others like you," the guy in Fargo had said, as if I were some kind of bird that was rarely seen in North Dakota.) But I did not know enough about my people, about our way of life and culture. Snatched away at age seven, I missed every single stage of growing up in a village in southern Sudan. I had begun my education as a man playing with other boys my age, making miniature cattle from clay, and throwing baby spears at dogs. But I had missed everything else that my people identified with growing up in Dinkaland: learning the knots to tie the cattle to their stakes for milking, taking over the care of my father's goats and then cattle, sitting with the other boys under a shady tree, teasing each other while the cattle grazed, making smoky fires from cattle dung to keep the mosquitoes away, while singing songs and telling riddles. Yes, I had sat for the marks of the Dinka Malwal to be carved onto my forehead. But it had happened in a refugee camp hundreds of miles away from my village. I had turned twenty without undergoing the traditional initiation rite that turns the Dinka boy of seventeen or eighteen into a man. Technically, I was still a boy. Any adult can send a boy on an errand. Boys cannot spend time with girls until they are initiated into manhood.

In a strange way, I was trying to become a Dinka in America; I was learning my customs among the Dinka of Iowa. I had no desire to talk to people from Boston about slavery. I threw the name and number away.

He called again and maybe again. I knew his name by heart: Jesse Sage. I ignored his messages. He even sent e-mails to Aguan, who had a computer and printed them out for me. I did not see any reason to tell this Jesse Sage from Boston what I was thinking: that I was okay in Ames, that I'm not a slave any more, that I have two jobs, that I'm not in Sudan, that I can't work with antislavery people in Boston. I tossed away the e-mails.

Then I got a call from Franco, who told me that the American Anti-Slavery Group was an important organization. He knew the man who had started it, Charles Jacobs, and he had spent time talking to Jesse Sage, who worked with Charles. They were doing important things to help our people. He revealed that he was the one who had told them about me, how he had helped this young ex-slave fill out his application to gain UN refugee status.

"It will be helpful not only for you to tell your story," Franco explained to me, "but you will also be able to speak on behalf of your people, those who are still suffering in the way that you did."

I could not refuse Franco, who had helped me change my life and was still helping refugees in the growing Dinka community in Lynn, a town north of Boston. But I told Franco I could not promise that I would work with this group. I had moved many times and knew how hard it was to get comfortable in a strange city. I had two good jobs. I was saving my money for school. I was even helping people in Cairo. I was working on my English. I still had my dream of being somebody in this world, somebody important. In Ames, I was in a position to improve my life. Why would I want to move to Boston and start all over again?

"I will go and visit and see what they are doing," I told Franco, who gave me Jesse Sage's phone number. I called him, told him I would talk, but he had to call me on the weekend when I had more time. When he called back, Jesse asked me some questions about my story, and we talked for about an hour. He explained that his organization, the American Anti-Slavery Group, was created to give survivors of slavery a chance to speak out. The group had already worked with a slave from Mauritania and a Dinka woman who had escaped two slave raids and was now living in the Boston area. After hearing about my story from Franco, the AASG thought that I could help them get Americans to do more to help the Dinka people of Sudan. After hearing me confirm that I had been a slave for ten years, this Jesse Sage told me that I could make their fight against slavery in Sudan more powerful than it had ever been. He was only an American who was outraged by slavery, while I was someone who had not only witnessed slavery with my own eyes but had lived it for ten years.

"We want to help you tell your story," he said, adding that he would like me to come visit them in Boston to find out more about their work. I had my job, I told him. He suggested that if I traveled to Boston on a Friday after work and returned Sunday evening, I would not have to miss any work. AASG would make all the travel arrangements and buy me the ticket. All I had to do was get to the plane on time.

When I got off the plane at the Boston airport after midnight, I was surprised to find such a young guy waiting for me. This abolitionist American turned out to be only two years older than I was. Jesse Sage took me to his apartment where I met his roommates, who talked about what I should see on my first trip to Boston, while Jesse fed me scrambled eggs so mushy that I asked if I could cook them some more. (I don't think he liked that.) I spent the night on his sofa bed. (That was something I didn't like.)

The next morning, we visited Harvard Square, a place filled with shops and students, and then walked through Harvard Yard, where Jesse began asking me a lot of questions about my life in Sudan. The UN and INS people had asked me questions about my story, Franco had grilled me to make sure I was telling it straight, but no one had ever asked me things like, "What were you thinking?", "What was going on in your mind when that happened?" I had a lot of answers.

Jesse led me into a big building nearby that was filled with only books, "the second largest library in America," he pointed out. I had never seen a library before, and I was amazed that one building could hold so many books—all of which I could not read. Inside he showed me a display of what Harvard looked like when the university was founded hundreds of years before, what it looked like in the nineteenth century, and again what it looked like seventy years ago.

I did not care. I had never heard of Harvard. I had never even been to elementary school. I preferred Jesse's suggestion to get a sandwich at a Harvard Square student hangout, where he told me more about the group's efforts to publicize what was happening in Sudan and try to get the American government to do something about it.

"You could help us a lot," Jesse said. I only nodded my head. Maybe I could help them, but I was not about to move from Ames, Iowa. I was sure of that. After lunch Jesse took me by subway to the AASG headquarters and showed me around the offices, which looked like all the other offices I had seen in Cairo, Fargo, and Ames: desks, chairs, computers, and lots of paper. (The Burke employee who cleaned the machines, not to mention the Holiday Inn housekeeper that I was, had an urge to tidy things up.)

Then I saw the pictures on the walls—pictures of Dinka people and Dinka villages. There were photographs of boys displaying the scars on their wrists rubbed raw and bloody from being tied up with rawhide. I had those same scars from that night Giemma had caught me escaping and promised to kill me. There was even a picture of a teenage boy with one arm. Jesse explained that the boy had been shot in the arm during a slave raid in 1995. One of the militia had tied him to his horse and dragged him along the ground until his injured arm was torn off, and then left him for dead. The boy, however, survived to be photographed as proof of the cruelty of the murahaliin. I stared at the picture and he stared back, photographed from the waist up, his chest bared to the camera, a healthy Dinka, with two strong shoulders—but only one arm. He had the face of a Dinka about my age, but the sad eyes of an old man. I looked at the kids with the scarred wrists and again at the one-armed kid. I had seen those empty eyes before on the boys at the watering places, kids who had stopped smiling. When I looked into the eyes of those photographed boys, I saw myself.

But on the wall of the AASG office there were also pictures of my people smiling into the camera, women and boys bouncing with life. The reason for their joy, Jesse explained, was that they had just been released from slavery. The AASG was working with another group in Europe, a Christian organization willing to pay money to purchase the freedom of slaves.[3] Those faces also moved me. They were Dinka, like me, who had been enslaved. But unlike me they did not have to risk their lives to escape. They were freed through the help of the AASG and the Europeans who bought people their freedom.

These were pictures of the real Sudan, of the Sudan that I knew. For the first time since I had heard from Jesse, I realized that maybe this group was doing something important after all. Suddenly, I saw myself helping my people. I had sat in Egypt and then in Fargo wondering what good I might do for southern Sudan now that I was free. Jesse was giving me the answer.

---

[3] Christian Solidarity International is based in Switzerland and works through a network of Arab Muslim "retrievers," men who pose as slave owners eager to add to their stock, buy the slaves, and then turn them over to CSI for $35–$75 each (the market equivalent of two goats). Sometimes CSI is able to make a deal with Arab chiefs; on rare occasions, retrievers are able to grab an unattended slave and take him or her to freedom.

The next day Jesse took me to meet Charles Jacobs, who founded AASG in 1993. Charles explained how he had read a story in the newspaper about slavery in Sudan. This fact stunned him. He had thought slavery was a thing of the past. But a little research proved him wrong: there were 27 million slaves in the world, and he decided he had to do something about it. He quit his job and used his savings to start a group to oppose slavery. I was amazed by this: one newspaper story, and this American changed his life to help people like me. Would I have done that? I liked Charles. He was friendly and easygoing. Jesse urged me to tell my story again to Charles. My English was terrible, but with Jesse's help I was able to tell it well. Jesse and I were like a team devoted to explaining what had happened to me. Charles just listened. What I was telling him was exactly what he had read about and heard from his friends who had talked to other slaves.

"So, Francis," Charles said to me. "We want you to come work with us."

I said nothing. All I remember is shaking my head. I didn't want to hear this.

"We want you to be part of our team," said Charles. He said he'd help me move to Boston, that he'd find me "financial support." He told me that he would help me tell my story to important people who could then help my own people in Africa. "You will help us tell the story of slavery in Sudan more powerfully," he said. "Don't worry about your English."

I said nothing. I was not sure I understood everything that he said, but it was clear that they wanted me to move to Boston and work with them. I just shook my head. I was worried about my English. I liked my life in Ames, my friends. I had come to

Boston because Franco told me I should. I was also curious
about what an antislavery group did. But I didn't want to disrupt
my life again. I had my jobs, my income, my dream of going to
school. I explained my reservations to Charles. How would I live
in Boston and support myself? What would they do for me?

Charles replied that the AASG would find me a place to stay;
they would support me financially. "You said you wanted to go
to school," he reminded me. Charles had pressed an important
button. "We can help you do that." School was my new dream.
But there were schools in Iowa. I was still shaking my head. I did
not want to say yes. But then I heard Charles say:

"Are you ready to come here?"

I was not ready. But the events of the day flashed in my
head—the pictures of the boys with the scars and the kid whose
arm had been ripped off, the smiling women and children who
had been freed, Charles's explanation of why he was devoting
himself to freeing slaves like me.

"Yes," I heard myself say. Suddenly, I was agreeing to do what
I was telling myself I did not want to do. But they needed me—
Charles, Jesse, and the slaves still in northern Sudan. No one had
ever said that they needed me. I had told myself that now that I
was free, I wanted to do some good. My father had always told
me that I would be an important person. Here was my chance.

Charles and Jesse seemed surprised by my quick commitment to return, but not as surprised as I was. Jesse asked me
how soon I could make the move.

"In a week," I said. I would go back to Ames, quit my jobs,
get my things together, say goodbye to my friends, and return
to Boston. I did not want to give myself too much time to
change my mind.

. . .

On May 14, 2000, I was on a plane back to Boston. I had said good-bye to Adel, Dau Dau, Aguan Aguan, and as many other of the friends I had made among the Dinka of Iowa. At first they could not believe that I was going to move to Boston. "You've got a good situation here," they said. "You're making good money." Others also warned me that the Sudanese government would not be happy about a South Sudanese talking in public. "This is a dangerous thing you are doing."

About all of this my friends were right. I was taking a big risk by leaving behind so many friends; and there were real dangers—which Charles and Jesse had probably not considered. They were eager to use my story to publicize their cause. That same publicity would invite the kind of danger that I had worked so hard and long to put behind me. But I had to do it. I tried to explain to my friends in Ames that I did not want to work in a meatpacking plant and clean rooms for the Holiday Inn for the rest of my life. Hadn't they told me to take advantage of the freedoms America offered, to go for the opportunities it gave, even for penniless refugees like us? Didn't they tell me to get an education? I saw Boston as my next step in realizing my two new dreams: to get an education and to do something that would help our people by telling my story. Charles had promised that he would help me go to school. He also said the AASG would pay for my expenses, and when I began going out on my own to tell my story in public, I would get paid. I wanted to do something important with my life, and I saw my work with the AASG as a step in that direction.

Also, this American Anti-Slavery Group was working with

people in Sudan who helped free slaves. Maybe these people could find out something about my parents.

I spent my first nights in Boston on Jesse's sofa bed. I was amazed by Jesse, this American kid only two years older than I, who was as passionate about ending slavery as I was, but knew much more about the history and politics of my country. I had to go to school to catch up with these American kids. But first I needed a place to live. Charles found me a room in a neighbor's home. For the next three or four months I would live with Dr. Dick Bales and his wife, Lynn, who were not only interested in Africa but had visited there. They gave me my own room and treated me as a member of their family. I ate dinner with them almost every evening. I also started working for the AASG, learning about their efforts to alert Americans about slavery in Sudan. Jesse was building a Web site for the organization—www.iAbolish.com—and I was trying to read some of the information they had compiled about the war in Sudan.

And then, only about a week after my move to Boston, Charles announced that he had arranged for me to tell my story to the Southern Baptist church in Roxbury.

"Just tell them what happened to you," he said, explaining that my audience would be mainly African Americans who, once they heard my story, would be eager to help in the fight against modern slavery. They would tell other churches about me, Charles said, pointing out that African-American Christians could be a powerful ally. Jesse and he would help me prepare what I would say.

I needed the right clothes. I could not speak to the Baptists in Roxbury about my life in slavery looking like a refugee from a hip-hop video on MTV. (I think Charles and Jesse were quite amused by my T-shirts and big jeans, baseball caps and train-

ing suits, and different pairs of sneakers.) I did not have a
jacket or tie; I didn't even have a shirt I could wear with a tie.
Charles had one of the interns from the office—the AASG
always has a lot of college students helping out—take me to a
Men's Wearhouse in the neighborhood for a jacket, pants, and
shirt. I found a brown jacket that I liked and black pants, but
then there was this problem: Every shirt that fit my arms was
much too big for my skinny neck. When we returned to the
AASG offices without a shirt, Jesse took me to a "Big Man"
shop that was also close by. Since I was tall but not so big—I
weighed about one hundred fifty pounds—they, too, could not
come up with a shirt that fit me properly. "You're going to have
shirts custom-made," the salesman informed us. It was a pretty
funny situation. Charles and Jesse were fighting slavery in the
world; they met with rich Americans to raise money and
talked to important politicians, but they couldn't find me a
shirt to wear. Jesse took me back to the Men's Wearhouse,
where they managed to find me a short-sleeved shirt that also
fit snugly around my neck.

My next challenge was breakfast with a newspaper reporter.
Jesse had arranged for us to meet Charles Radin from the *Boston
Globe*, who had done a story the year before about an escaped
slave from Mauritania who had also worked with the AASG.
The deal was that Radin would interview me, attend my talk at
the Baptist Church, and then write a story. We met in a diner in
Brookline, where I had my first interview and my first waffle
breakfast. The Globe reporter asked me a lot of questions about
my life. My English was still sketchy, and I didn't understand
many of the things he was saying. Once again, Jesse helped us
get things straight. As the reporter left the diner I heard him say,

"You know, Jesse, I can only do these escaped slave stories once a year." I didn't understand what he meant. Slavery was wrong. It was an evil that the American people opposed. If there were 27 million slaves in the world, shouldn't there be a story in the newspaper every day condemning that fact?

It was a Sunday morning communion service, and the Southern Baptist Church was packed with parishioners and others who had heard that this "ex-slave" would be speaking. Charles had driven me to the church and introduced me to the pastor, Gerald Bell, an African-American man who was a friend of his and on the board of the AASG. Someone took a picture of us. I was very nervous. I had never stood in front of so many people I did not know. To be speaking in a church was also strange. I wanted to do a good job for Charles and Jesse, but I also felt that God was watching me, too. Pastor Bell spoke to his mostly African-American congregation: "Young people, you need to hear this! It was once this way with us."

"Amen," replied some of the people.

"We were slaves, and no one wanted to believe us," said the pastor. "Yes, Lord!"

It was now my turn. I took a deep breath and apologized for my bad English. And then I told them about that day when I went to the marketplace to sell my mother's beans and eggs, when the militia attacked and I was taken away to work for Giemma Abdullah for ten years, never to see my family again. Charles and Jesse had helped me get it down on paper, but I spoke from my heart and the church was silent. When I finished everyone began clapping and cheering. I looked out over their faces, smiling and crying. It was a strange feeling to be the center of so much attention—and emotion. My story had stirred up feelings in my audience, which I could now feel coming back at me.

Charles smiled at me and signaled that I had done a good job. Pastor Bell asked everyone to come out of their seats and gather around me closely. "Touch him!" he said. "Lift up this brother! Support him! Give him strength!" Everyone obeyed, surrounding me, reaching out and laying their hands on me.

"We will help your people," they promised. "Don't feel isolated here, we will take care of you." They said, "Think of us as your family." It was literally thrilling for me to be welcomed by all these American black faces, descendants of slaves who wanted to help me and the Dinka people. Afterwards people came up to me and shook my hand. "This happened to our ancestors," they said, "and we will respond to your call for help."

The next day at the office I described to Jesse how amazing it was for me to talk to those African-Americans, for them to lay their hands on me, to pledge their help. Charles told him I was a "big hit"—and then he gave me another surprise. "Tomorrow we are going to Washington, D.C.," Charles announced. "You are going to speak on Capitol Hill."

Looking back on that moment and knowing so much more now than I did then, I don't think I understood that sentence at all. By then I had lived in the United States long enough to know that "Washington, D.C." was the American capital. I had watched the television news, but I had no idea about how the American government actually worked. I had been too busy in Fargo and Ames trying to earn my living and understand what my bosses were saying. That I myself would actually go to the center of the American government and tell my story was inconceivable to me.

Charles, of course, had anticipated my anxiety. He explained that for months the AASG had been working with several other groups on "The Sudan Campaign," an effort to alert Americans in general, but politicians in particular, about slavery in Sudan. Charles himself had spent most of the month in Washington organizing the event that would include an opening meeting in the same building where the Congress met. Several people would be speaking, and he wanted me to be one of them.[4]

---

[4] In 1998, Freedom House, the nation's oldest human rights organization, initiated "Sudan Campaign of Conscience," attracting other groups concerned about human rights abuses in Sudan. By the time I went to Washington in 2000 to take part in what was now called the Sudan Campaign, the AASG had worked with Freedom House to bring together an extraordinary coalition of groups on all sides of the political spectrum for a series of formal weekly meetings and coordinated events that took place over several months, plus efforts to pressure Congress for a strong U.S. stand against the violence and slavery going on in Sudan: the Urban League, Salvation Army, American Jewish Committee, Family Research Council, Hudson Institute, Heritage Foundation, Institute on Religion and Democracy, Southern Baptist Convention, U.S. Catholic Conference, Catholic Relief Services, The A. Phillip Randolph Institute, Ethics and Public Policy Center, International Christian Concern, Persecution Project, Peter's Voice, Prison Fellowship Ministries, Religious Action Center for Reform Judaism, Samaritan's Purse, Servant's Heart, U.S. Holocaust Memorial Museum, U.S. Committee of Refugees, and World Vision. The other speakers were also a politically diverse group: Sen. Sam Brownback (R-KS) and Representatives Donald Payne (D-NJ), Joseph Pitts (R-PA), Tom Tancredo (R-CO), Barbara Lee (D-CA), John Lewis (D-GA), Frank Wolf (R-VA), Ben Gilman (R-NY), Ed Royce (R-CA), John Conyers (D-MI), along with Eleanor Holmes Norton, the Washington, D.C. representative and former civil rights lawyer, Joe Madison, the nationally-syndicated African-American talk show host, and John Eibner of Christian Solidarity International, the Swiss-based antislavery group that had been rescuing slaves in Sudan.

I resisted the idea. My English was not good enough. Charles insisted: I was great at the Baptist church, he said, and he assured me that all I had to do in Washington was repeat what I had done in Roxbury.

Early the next morning we were on the Delta shuttle to Washington, with Charles and Jesse trying to explain to me what the U.S. Congress did. I didn't understand a word. I knew nothing about politics, never mind democratic politics, American style. I had no idea what I was in for, or its magnitude. By eleven I was inside one of Congress's biggest meeting rooms, sitting with a group of African-American ministers, members of congress, and a U.S. Senator, watching Charles introduce us to an audience of about five hundred people. That this was important I now understood. As soon as I entered the room, reporters came up to interview me. Some were armed with cameras and huge microphones aimed at me. I was led to a table where I saw "Francis Bok" printed on a card next to another that said, "Joe Madison," who I later discovered had his own radio show. For me, it was truly an unreal experience. Pyo, too, was there—the man I had lived with in Cairo, the first to tell me that I should apply for UN refugee status. I had told Charles he was in the Washington area, and Charles invited him to speak. It was great to see Pyo again, and we embraced, marveling at the circumstances of this meeting so far from Cairo. Sultan Pyo and Francis on Capitol Hill, speaking to five hundred people. Who in Cairo would have believed this?

As the first speaker began, I looked at my audience: so many adults, well-dressed, important-looking, so many people from the media, reporters, photographers, TV cameras, and I began to feel much more nervous than I had been at the

Baptist church. I realized that I felt more than just the fear of
speaking in front of strangers in bad English. The last time I
went around telling my story in public I was arrested by the
secret police. And even though I was far from Khartoum, I was
about to say the one thing that the government in Khartoum
did not want people to know. In Washington. Before the press
and TV cameras.

There were also Arabs in the audience.

I was aware of the dangers of speaking out. Going to the
AASG offices to educate myself about the politics of Sudan,
even giving a speech to strangers, was easier than making pallets, cleaning meatpacking machines or rooms in the Holiday
Inn. But the struggle against slavery was a more dangerous
job. Charles and Jesse informed me that sometimes the office
got threatening letters and phone calls, mainly from northern
Sudanese Arabs in the U.S. who angrily claimed that there was
no slavery in Sudan. There had been spies in the camps in
Khartoum, and I was sure there were spies in Washington.
What was said in that room—and probably my name and
picture—would be reported back to the government of Sudan.[5]

Still, I had accepted the consequences of my new job. By
agreeing to work with the AASG, I had decided that my safety
was not as important as informing Americans about slavery in
Sudan. On the walls of the meeting room, someone had hung

[5] Dr. Hamouda Fathelrahman spoke after me. Secretary-General of the
Cairo-based Sudan Human Rights Organization, he is one of the few northern Sudanese who is an outspoken opponent of the war against the south.
His organization had published a report on slavery in Sudan. Khartoum
would not ignore our "Campaign for Sudan."

enlarged pictures of Dinka victims, pictures like the ones that had moved me so much when I first visited the AASG offices in Boston. Those images of escaped slaves, of Dinka hurt badly by bombings and mutilated by their slave owners reminded me how important it was to tell the Americans of the terrible things that were happening to my people. My decision had been made. But as I stood there in that room on Capitol Hill, my stomach tightening and sweat dripping through my short-sleeved shirt (it was too hot for the tie), I realized that my body had not yet accepted the conclusion my mind had come to. I was so afraid that I appealed to God for help. "Give me the strength to do this," I prayed.

When Charles introduced me I approached the podium with the two-page statement that Jesse had helped me prepare. I looked out over the audience, all these important Washington people who had come to hear about slavery in Sudan. I realized that this was a subject I knew better than any of them. I didn't have to read my story to them. I already had it in my heart, and so, with God's help, the words came out. I told them how I was kidnapped and was forced to work for Giemma for ten years until I was able to escape. I told them how they had beaten me and treated me like an animal. As I spoke, cameras flashed at me, but I also noticed something else: the silence in the room full of all of these important people listening to me. I called on the American people, especially my African-American brothers and sisters, to stand up and help my people. And then I thanked them for letting me speak.

It was over. I had spoken on Capitol Hill. I had survived.

And then the clapping started. They clapped and then stood up from their seats and kept clapping. Though in the past I had felt embarrassed by applause, I had never heard such a sound, and I had never felt so proud. Five hundred Americans on their feet, clapping for a 21-year-old boy from southern Sudan.

When the clapping stopped, a man came over and shook my hand; several African-American ministers joined him.[6] They thanked me for telling them about slavery in my country. To them, slavery had been something that happened in a far-off place in Africa they rarely gave a moment's thought to. After my speech, slavery had become a person they had seen, a young Sudanese whose hand they had actually shaken. When we left the building, I saw a few Arab protestors handing out leaflets that denied the existence of slavery in Sudan.

Back in Boston, Jesse showed me a copy of the *Boston Globe*. I was amazed. There on the second page of Boston's most important newspaper was a big picture of me in the church, under the headline:

BEARING WITNESS TO THE SCARS OF SLAVERY:
SURVIVOR'S TALE RAISES AMERICAN AWARENESS
OF BONDAGE IN SUDAN

With all the excitement about Washington, I had forgotten about the *Globe* interview. The paper had chosen to run the story about my appearance at the Southern Baptist Church on the same day I was speaking in Washington. The story took up almost half the page. I tried to read it, but all I could make out

---

[6] I did not know who these people were. But Jesse later informed me that the first to shake my hand was Sen. Sam Brownback from Kansas, and one of the ministers was T. D. Jakes, a famous African-American pastor with a big church and a popular television show. A year later, Jesse showed me the Reverend Jakes's picture on the cover of *Time* magazine, which had named him "America's best preacher."

were several words that I said. The message, however, was clear to me: What I had done at the church and then on Capitol Hill was important enough for a big newspaper and U.S. Senators to pay attention to an ex-slave who had never been to school.

On June 5, I was back in Washington for the final two days of The Sudan Campaign. We began with a morning press conference at the Lincoln Memorial featuring the STOP Slavery Campaign, a group of fifth-grade kids from Denver, Colorado, whose teacher, Barbara Vogel, had read them a newspaper article about Sudanese slavery. They decided they had to do something about this: They wrote letters to Washington, raised money, and were featured on the CBS news. And because people in power were not answering their pleas over the next year, they decided to go to Washington and find out why. On our way to the Lincoln Memorial, Jesse explained to me that Abraham Lincoln had been the U.S. President who had freed the slaves, and had been willing to risk a civil war to do it.

I will never forget that day: The Lincoln Memorial was white and gleaming in the sun, the little American kids so excited about being there, a few of them nervous about speaking in public. I spoke for a few minutes, telling my story once again and thanking these American kids who lived comfortable lives that never required them to think about the terrible things happening in Sudan, but were working hard to publicize those horrors. When I finished the kids came up and hugged me and shook my hand. Some of them had tears streaming down their cheeks. I had now told my story in the church in Roxbury and on Capitol Hill. But that day, after speaking in front of a memorial to an American leader who had freed the slaves in his country, as I was hugged by those kids with tears in their eyes I began to understand how powerful words could be.

The kids were scheduled to visit several congressmen, including their own representative, Republican Tom Tancredo. I also remember sitting around the office of Rep. Donald Payne, the New Jersey Democrat who was the leader of the Black Caucus in Congress, and, as he told the kids how happy he was about the work they were doing, I thought about how amazing it was that this man whose ancestors had been slaves was now a powerful American. Could this ever happen in Sudan?

We had gone from the Lincoln Memorial to the congressional offices, and then from office to office. At one point, a girl from the class took my hand and we walked together. Christy was her name. She came up to my waist, and while it must've looked to others that I was leading this little girl around town, Christy, in fact, had taken my hand. Why? I am not sure. To me, though, it was an example of how easy it was for different people to live with each other: All you have to do is reach out and take their hand.

We ended up in a room with a long table that had a sign at each chair with a name on it. Jesse explained to me that this was a special room for meetings of a group of powerful senators who worked on problems in foreign countries.[7] The kids were still pretty excited. I was tired. Suddenly an old man entered the room, using a cane to walk. He shook the hands of all the kids and mine, too. His name was Jesse Helms. The

---

[7] The Senate Foreign Relations Committee caucus room. The committee chairman at the time was Jesse Helms, the Senator from North Carolina.

kids explained why they had come to Washington. In Sudan, kids like me had been enslaved, and the rest of the world was not doing anything about it. I told him what had happened to me. He just listened, but I could see the emotion in his eyes. I was not sure his tears were for the slaves in Sudan or a reaction to all that emotion in the room, but after we spoke, he hugged the kids and shook my hand with tears still in his eyes. "I promise you," he said, "that we will help your people."

Mr. Helms also said that he wanted the kids and me to come back to Washington and testify before his committee. He had also set up a meeting for us at the State Department with the Secretary of State, Madeline Albright. We all trooped over to that building, but Albright was not available. Instead, we were greeted by the woman in charge of Africa.[8] I talked to her about my situation, and the kids got to restate their concern that the U.S. was not doing enough about slavery in Sudan.

"Why isn't President Clinton speaking out against this?" the kids asked. The Assistant Secretary of State said she would bring their message to Madeline Albright. She also assured us that President Clinton was very concerned about slavery in Sudan and would speak out about it soon. She thanked us for coming.

As we left her office, I thought about how strange and amazing all of this was. When my UN interviewer in Egypt had asked me what country I wanted to go to, I said I didn't care; I just wanted to be free. Many Sudanese wanted to come to America, and once I got here and saw how rich everyone was, I thought that I finally understood what the attraction of America was. But during those two days in Washington

---

[8] Susan Rice, Assistant Secretary of State for African Affairs.

I learned what was really amazing about America: Important senators and experts on Africa would not only give their time to a group of schoolchildren and a refugee from Sudan, but what we said could bring tears to their eyes. In Sudan, when I told the truth in Jabarona, the secret police threw me in jail; even in Cairo, where we were free to say what we wanted in the streets, no one with real political power was listening to us southern Sudanese who had run away from hell. When I moved to Boston, I was not sure that one uneducated Dinka boy could really accomplish much. But after my two trips to Washington, D.C., I began to think that maybe Francis Bok, from the village of Gourion, Aweil Province, southern Sudan, could actually make things better for his people.

Speaking in Washington was a major turning point in my life—but not just because I got a chance to tell my story to important people or even influenced them about U.S. relations with Sudan. That first day on Capitol Hill, I finally met the man responsible for those smiling faces on the Dinka women and children in the photograph in the AASG offices. John Eibner, a director of Christian Solidarity International who has dedicated his life to helping my people, was also one of the speakers at The Sudan Campaign rally. He is an extraordinary human being, one of those rare people who are both great and humble. I had heard many Christians talk about the importance of "loving your neighbor." John's life is a daily example of Christian love. Before I could finish thanking him for his help, he was already helping me. John told me that he would be returning to southern Sudan soon, to the Aweil area, and if I gave him the name of my parents and my village, he would try to get some news of my family.

CHAPTER SEVENTEEN

NEWS FROM SUDAN

My nervous, halting efforts to get my message across in Washington convinced me that I had to work much harder on my English. I reminded Charles and Jesse that they had promised to help me go to school. Jesse made a lot of phone calls and soon discovered that finding a school for a 21-year-old without any formal education would not be easy. Enrolling in an ordinary elementary school was out of the question. As eager as I was for education, I was not about to go to school with little kids who came up to my hip, even if a school would have me, which was doubtful. And no high school was willing to take me because I was so uneducated and so old. I also needed a place I could attend class in the evenings, so that during the day I could work for the AASG. Jesse came up with a list of schools in Boston that could help me with my English, and I began checking them out.

I had been focused so much on improving my English and trying to find a school those first few months in Boston that I had forgotten about John Eibner's trip to Sudan—until he called me at the office. During his June visit to Sudan, as he had promised, he had gone to my village and located a man who was part of my father's clan and had known my family well. John had informed him that I was alive and well in America and was eager to find out what happened to my parents and sisters. John had videotaped his answer and played the audio over the telephone, so I could hear what this clansman of mine had said: That same day the militia had attacked the marketplace in Nyamlell, they had also raided my own village. My father had been killed. He seemed sure of that. He also believed that my mother and two sisters were gone, too. He said he was very happy that I had survived and was safe in the United States. John said he would send me a photograph of this man who knew my family.

I thanked John for his help. My dream of twelve years had been shattered by a few minutes on the phone. I don't remember putting down the phone, or what I did next. My head was too full of thoughts—all guilt, anger, sadness, and confusion about what to do. I realized that I had been spending so much time getting my life in order in Boston and working on the issue of slavery in Sudan that I had given little thought to my own family. For many years, when I thought about my father he was alive and present to me. But all that time I was dreaming about returning to his house, about being picked up onto his shoulders, he did not exist; my father had been dead the entire time I was with Giemma. And I was alive. It was hard for me to accept that I would never see my father again. I prayed to God for his soul, and I thanked my father for all he had given me as a child—and as a slave.

I now had to face up to the reality that my mother and sisters, too, were dead. The man John had talked to believed they, too, were dead, and I decided that I would believe him. What about my older brother? The day I went to the market he was not at home; for weeks he had been visiting relatives in another village far from us. Was that village attacked? Was he dead, too? I assumed the worst. I looked around the office. The AASG people were doing their work, helping my people. They were talking and laughing and making plans for the evening. They had no idea my parents were dead. I had spent almost thirteen years assuming they were alive. Or had I? I never remember thinking that they might have died in a raid that same day the murahaliin attacked the marketplace. When the militia divided us kids up, I wanted to be with my parents. Sitting on Giemma's big horse, riding through the black night, I cried for my mother. When I got to Giemma's and his kids beat me up, I cried for my parents. Those first nights alone, sleeping near the animals, I was sure my parents would come and rescue me. And virtually every day for the next ten years, I lived to see my family again.

I never thought that they were dead. I couldn't think that. If someone had told me that first day that my parents were dead, I would have gone crazy. Sitting there in the AASG offices with the burden of John Eibner's bad news sitting on my chest, I realized that my parents had saved my life. Without my dream of getting them back, I never would have had the will to survive my life with Giemma and his family. I might have tried to escape when I was too young. I might have done something stupid, said something that would have got my arm chopped off. I certainly would not have been so cooperative with Giemma to get him to play my double game.

I did not cry over my parents' death. Why? Because I was

not surprised. No Dinka my age who had lived in Khartoum and Cairo, or even in the south Sudanese communities of Fargo, Ames, Manchester, or Lynn could be shocked by the death of family and friends during the past fifteen years. I had truly believed that I would find my family—until I arrived in the refugee camps of Khartoum. In Jabarona and elsewhere I had quickly discovered that my story of violence and loss was shared by millions of Dinka. Everyone I met had lost friends and family. It was then that I began to face up to the probability that I might never see my parents again. I don't remember saying that to myself; I don't remember thinking it through so clearly. But, by the time I heard the bad news from John Eibner, it came as no surprise. It was a shock, but the shock of the inevitable, what I had been steeling myself to face over the past four years. For me, it was another reason to hate the government of Sudan: Not only had they allowed my parents to be killed, such violence multiplied by the two million Dinka killed in southern Sudan over almost twenty years had deprived me of the tears to cry over my own loss. They had made me such a survivor that it was almost too easy for me to survive the news that my parents were dead.

But they lived in my memory. I could still feel their love toward me. I was grateful that they had given me life, both as a baby and as a young man. But that day I heard the bad news from Sudan in the AASG offices in Boston, I realized that I had to go on with my life without parents. I had to find another dream.

CHAPTER EIGHTEEN

THE EDUCATION OF FRANCIS BOK

I tried to lose myself in my schoolwork. I had enrolled in a class at the Jewish Vocational Services that Jesse told me about, in which I could work on my English while also picking up some computer skills. It struck me as a useful combination. Even someone as unschooled as I about the modern world could see that computers would be as useful to me as the English language. I would be able to use the computers in the office to keep in touch with my friends in Ames by e-mail. But most important: Jewish Vocational Services was the only school that would accept me. I enrolled.

I found it difficult. Just being in school was tough for me, sitting in a classroom and trying to understand what they were saying. It took all the powers of concentration I had to focus on listening to instructions I barely understood. I spent most of my first summer in Boston in that class, which turned out to be more about computers than English, which we worked on only one day a week. I did learn how to type, and I also developed some skill with Microsoft Word, Excel, and PowerPoint presentations. But I soon realized that I had little in common with my fellow students besides poor English. They were mainly adults with their own families. Most of my classmates had been to school before. They already knew how to read and write. Some had even been to university in their own countries and were eager to learn computer skills to get a better job. I had a job, and it didn't make sense to me to try to improve my English among people whose English was as bad, or even worse, than mine. Boston was filled with recent immigrants—Russians, Serbs, Mexicans, Asians, as well as other Africans—but when you asked them about school, all they could talk about was "ESL"—English as a Second Language schools. I was convinced that my English would improve faster if I was in class with native English speakers. (Wasn't that the way I had learned Arabic so quickly?) I was also eager to learn things besides English—history, math, and science. I wanted to be educated about what was going on in the world. I wanted to be able to read books. To be effective at the AASG, to help change life in Sudan, I needed more than computer literacy or even fluency in English—I needed knowledge.

Then Jesse told me about the Boston Evening Academy. A friend of a friend of his taught there, said Jesse, and it sounded like a perfect school for me: afternoon and evening classes, lots of different kids, mainly high school drop-outs with varied educational backgrounds, most of them working while trying to finish high school. I would be required to take courses in history and culture, math and science, and English—literature, not ESL. Better still, the government supported the school, which meant I could attend for free.

On enrollment day in September 2000, I showed up at the Boston Evening Academy to find a series of tables where I was told I could sign up for various courses. I went to the first table—and I was already stuck: I had no idea how to fill out the form. One of the staff—"My name is Michelle," she said with a smile—offered to help me. It turned out that for me there was no choice in what I had to study. I needed the basics: science and technology, mathematics, "humanities" (history and English literature), and "personal development," whatever that was.

The next day I sat in a real school for the first time in my life. I was twenty-one going on twenty-two. I was also extremely excited. But the experience turned out to be strange and upsetting.

"How tall are you?" the other kids asked.

"Six foot six." They laughed at my voice and accent. And when I asked questions in class, they laughed even more. When I admitted having trouble reading and writing, they were amazed—and laughed at me some more.

"Why did you never learn to read or write?" they asked.

I told them that I had never been to school in my entire life.

"Why not?" they asked. "What happened?"

I didn't want to get into all of that. I didn't want to have to explain life in Sudan, the war, the crazy politics. I barely understood it all myself, but I knew they wouldn't care. They hadn't even heard of Sudan. These were American kids, a mixed group of white, black, Hispanic, and Asian teenagers, mainly American-born, who had dropped out of school or got kicked out. The oldest were seventeen or eighteen. I could tell from their behavior in class—the joking, teasing, and fooling around—that they were not like the college kids who worked at the AASG, who cared about what was happening in Africa. American kids seemed to be able to say whatever they wanted to and get away with it. Outside of class they broke the rules and bragged about it. They made fun of the teachers, so it was not surprising they would make fun of the new African kid who was older and taller than they were, but a lot stupider and talked with a funny voice and accent. All I had to do was say something in incorrect English and they would laugh. One guy would imitate my voice and accent and poor English usage, and the others would laugh as if he were the funniest man on earth.

I wanted to pound them into the ground.

But I resisted the urge to play their game. I warned myself: "You must control your feelings, even when they say something mean or cruel to you. These are American kids who have lived this wonderful life." I wanted to tell them how lucky they were. I had heard that American kids get to start school at three years old. And here were these kids who, even though they had quit school or had gotten kicked out, were given another chance to finish high school. Sometimes several chances. For free. I also wanted to tell them that I was ready to get educated, no matter how long it would take and no matter how much they teased me.

Still, the things they said about me stung. "See that guy— he's so stupid he can't even read." As I walked out of school every day kids would tease me and make fun of me, and I was very angry. But I also understood that their words did not hurt as much as Giemma's whip. The Boston Evening Academy was no refugee camp. I was happy to be there, in spite of these ignorant teenagers who talked about their TV shows, favorite music, and sports, but seemed to have no idea of the horrible things that went on in the rest of the world.

"Some day I will explain what happened to me," I said to a

THE EDUCATION OF FRANCIS BOK

couple of kids. "I can't talk about it now. I'm not able to explain it clearly. But some day I will explain why I have never been to school."

I did not tell anyone at school about my work with the American Anti-Slavery Group, about Washington, about the speeches I gave. I did not show them the big story about me in the *Boston Globe*.

Charles had been selected to receive the first annual "Boston Freedom Award," and he asked me to tell my story. The ceremony would take place at the Old South Meeting House in downtown Boston, where American abolitionists had struggled against slavery before the Civil War. The Mayor would be there, and Coretta Scott King, the widow of Martin Luther King, Jr., was scheduled to present the award to Charles. That Charles had asked me to speak I took as a great honor. It was, after all, Charles's night. Yet he made it an unforgettable evening for me, too. Martin Luther King's wife and I would be speaking at the same event! I had a lot to learn about America, but I knew who Martin Luther King, Jr. was. My roommate in Ames had a photograph of Dr. King on the wall. Charles, who had been a civil rights activist in the 1960s, explained that King was a famous African-American minister who had fought for the rights of black people in this country. He also screened the video for me of King's famous "I have a dream" speech, which I found very moving. I met Mrs. King at her hotel room and presented her with a photograph of Dinka women and children being released from slavery. "Keep helping your people," she said to me. "This is a gift God has given to you." She told me that her husband was a man dedicated to telling the truth, no matter the consequences. I couldn't wait to tell Aguan Aguan that I had met Dr. King's wife.

The Old South Meeting House was packed with five hundred or so people, many of them, according to Jesse, very famous in Boston. Many south Sudanese had also come to hear me speak. Again, Jesse had helped me with my speech, a slightly longer variation of my story adapted to the context of the historic fight against slavery fueled from Boston—and in this very building—where the abolitionists attacked the horror of men, women, and children being treated like animals. I was living proof that such horrors had not ended with the American Civil War in 1865.

Within another week, I was flying back to Washington to testify before the Senate Foreign Relations Committee. Senator Helms's staff had called to ask me to appear with five students from Barbara Vogel's class to urge the Senate to do more about slavery in Sudan. The kids spoke first, and one kid was brilliant. "My name is Dong Cho," he said. "I'm a student at Highline Community Elementary School in Aurora, Colorado. I have to go to school every day. And I have homework and chores to do at home. But I still have time to free slaves. Is Congress too busy?"

The entire room broke up. People clapped. It was the perfect comment. When my turn came, I told the committee how proud I was to speak to U.S. Senators on behalf of my people who were being killed and enslaved. I told them my story, about my kidnapping, my life with Giemma's family, how they fed me bad food and beat me and said I was an "animal," how for ten years I had no one to laugh with, for ten years I had no one to love me. I told them how I finally escaped when I was seventeen, only to be enslaved by the police. I told them how that Arab truck driver had taken me home with him and helped me get to Khartoum where I was jailed for months. I told them how I made my way to Cairo, became a UN refugee, and flew to the United States in 1999. I told them that the AASG found me in Iowa and asked me to come to work with them in Boston, where I was going to school for the first time in my life. Jesse and I had talked about how to make this speech a little different. Since I was with the fifth graders, we decided to remind the Senators that there are millions of children in the world still enslaved. Here's how I ended my speech:

I am a lucky man. I am free. But my people are dying. And around the world there are twenty-seven million slaves who cannot speak. Today I must speak for them.

Senators, we have a big question: "Why is President Clinton silent about slavery in Sudan? And why is the world silent?" This is a country that freed its slaves. People are still slaves. Will the United States come free us?

When I was living as a slave to Giemma Abdullah, I would lie awake at night. I could not sleep. I would think: "How am I going to be free? Is someone going to come and free me?"

Today in Sudan and around the world, there are children who cannot sleep at night. They lay on the ground and wait for strong people to come and get them. Senators, you are strong people. You have a big voice and strong arms. You can free the slaves!

Senators, I am here alone. I have no family here. But you— the people of the United States—are now my family. And I know you will free your brothers and sisters.

For all the people who are still slaves in Sudan, I say to you:
Thank you very much.

After the hearing we visited Senator Helms in his office, where
I met his wife. He arranged another meeting for us at the State
Department, and this time we did meet with Madeline
Albright, the U.S. Secretary of State—a nice woman who actu-
ally seemed to listen to what we were saying as we urged her
to persuade the Clinton Administration to make a formal state-
ment against slavery in Sudan. She assured us that the
President was concerned about what was going on in Sudan.

I also had dinner that night with Perry Farrell, the lead
singer for a rock group called "Jane's Addiction." I did not
know who Farrell was or why he was in Washington. Jesse
explained that the rock singer was friends with an antislavery
activist named Aaron Cohen who had brought him to the hearings. Someone told me that Perry cried during my testimony. "I
have to do something about this," he told me afterwards. Five of
Pyo's sons joined us at the restaurant, and we had a great time—
a bunch of Dinka guys who not so long ago had been desperate
refugees together in Cairo, now sitting at a table in an expensive
restaurant in the American capital with a rock star talking about
my testimony before the Senate Foreign Relations Committee
and a meeting with the U.S. Secretary of State.

America was an amazing country. I had been in the U.S.
for a little more than a year and I already had had my picture
in the *Boston Globe,* hung out with the Chairman of the Senate
Foreign Relations Committee and a rock star, and had my picture taken with Coretta Scott King *and* the Secretary of State.

Of all the dreams I had dreamt, I could never have imagined such things. But I had learned how important it was to have a dream, something to shoot for, to live for. I had escaped, come to America, and begun helping my people. My decision to come to Boston was the right one. Already, though, I had a new dream: to finish high school and go to college.

I worked hard in class at the Boston Evening Academy; I did my homework every day. My teachers were terrific, always helping. My humanities teacher, Ryan Oliver, who also happened to be the friend of Jesse's friend who told him about the Boston Evening Academy, became my adviser and took the job seriously. He would sit with me for hours over my schoolwork, one-on-one. Whenever I got frustrated over how much I had to learn to catch up with even my dimmest classmates, Mr. Oliver encouraged me. "If you keep working hard," he advised, "you'll be fine." The college interns at the AASG were always willing to answer my questions and help me with my math and various projects, which was basically kids' stuff for them. In my history class, for example, we started with Christopher Columbus and worked our way through world history. Every fact was a revelation to me: all these kings and queens and generals and explorers who kept changing the world. Centuries of history that we did not know about in Sudan. (At first this bothered me, until I realized through my political work with the AASG that there was so much going on in Africa that most Americans were ignorant about.) I asked lots of questions, more than my classmates for whom this was all familiar.

One afternoon, Mr. Martyn, my history teacher, pulled me aside after class. He had heard about my story, he said. He had even checked me out on the AASG Web site. He was aware that the other kids were making fun of me. "Ignore them," he said. "Some day I will tell them your story." Mr. Martyn encouraged me to keep asking questions in class. He also suggested that I write a paper about life in Sudan, how my people lived and worked. I agreed and went to work. Assembling information about daily life in southern Sudan reminded me of what I had left behind. It was my opportunity to educate the other students about a country they hadn't even heard of— even though it was the largest nation on the largest continent. I even did a big poster with photographs I found in the AASG office of Sudanese houses, cattle, and other customs. After I presented my project to the class, Mr. Martyn went on-line and accessed the AASG's Web site that featured my picture and news of the speeches I had given.

"This is him," he said to the class, pointing to my picture. They were amazed. All those kids who had made fun of me for being stupid could not believe that I had been a slave and was now was giving speeches about it to schools and Senators.

"Next time Francis speaks in the Boston area," Mr. Martyn announced to the class, "we will go and hear him."

My next speech, however, was in New York at the United Nations. Sudan was about to be elected to the UN Security Council, and the antislavery forces were going to hold a press conference at the UN in October attacking this outrage. Charles and I traveled to New York to speak. I presented myself as a living example of why Sudan was in no position to be a power in a world body devoted to peace. Once again,

I could not believe what I was doing. Here I was, an official UN Refugee standing outside the organization's headquarters in New York City, speaking on who should and should not be part of its most important ruling body.

And once again I helped change things: Shortly after our demonstration, Secretary of State Albright and the U.S. Ambassador to the UN, Richard Holbrooke, began a lobbying effort among the African delegates who eventually nominated Mauritius to the Security Council slot and not Sudan. The Sudan Campaign that had begun my first month in Washington and continued through the summer trying to stir up opposition to Khartoum's cruel regime had achieved a remarkable victory. One thing was also certain: I had created more enemies in Khartoum.

In December, I was scheduled to take part in a conference at Harvard, and I told Mr. Martyn about it. The student interns from Harvard working in the AASG offices had persuaded the Institute of Politics at Harvard's Kennedy School to hold a meeting on "Slave Trafficking in the Twenty-first Century." One of the Harvard students, Jay Williams, who had traveled to Sudan with John Eibner, would be talking. Jesse Sage would also speak, and I would tell my story. For the point of view from Washington, Harvard had invited the Clinton Administration's National Security Council's specialist on human trafficking, Wendy Patten.

Students were hanging from the rafters of the lecture hall. At least five hundred people—in front of us, up above us, all over the place. The room was filled with energy. Jesse described the sense of anticipation there as "electric." I, too, was excited, and when I looked out in the audience and saw

Mr. Martyn and the principal from Boston Evening Academy, Mr. Fried, along with almost a hundred students, I was even more eager to speak. We sat at a table behind cards with our names printed on them, just like in a Senate hearing. Jay Williams spoke about his experience helping free two thousand slaves in Sudan, I told my story—for the first time without any notes—and then Jesse tied things together by pointing out that one of the reasons that the U.S. Government had been silent about slavery in the world was that the American people had been silent.

The woman from the White House spoke last. She did not seem to be an expert on Sudan, and talked about the issue of slave trafficking in general. But she did insist that slavery in Sudan was a problem that concerned President Clinton. During the question period, some wondered why the Administration had not done more. Jesse expanded on his point that when the people don't complain to politicians, they are less likely to act; that most Americans did not even know that a civil war had been raging for decades in Sudan, nor about the existence of slavery. We had to let Washington know that we felt strongly about this issue, and he pointed out that we actually had a government representative with us that night. "You should send her a message that slavery is something that Americans will not stand for."

Wendy Patten was suddenly on the hot seat. One girl got up and identified herself as "a student at the Boston Evening Academy with Francis Bok."

"I want to tell the person from the White House," she said. "Why isn't President Clinton saying something about this? I don't understand that. He's got to say something. How can he be silent, when this happens to someone in my own school?"

Person after person stood up and repeated that criticism. You could feel the anger in the room. I began to feel sorry for the woman from the White House. But the message evidently got through to her. Four days later—Human Rights Day—President Clinton gave a speech in which, among other things, he said that the U.S. must speak out against human rights abuses in the world, citing in particular "the scourge of slavery in Sudan." He then seemed to praise the AASG efforts directly by saying: "Let me say especially to the students, religious communities, and human rights activists who have done so much to publicize the atrocities of Sudan: America must continue to press for an end to these egregious practices and make clear that the Sudanese government could not join the community of nations until fundamental changes are made on these fronts."

I was thrilled by Clinton's words. I had actually played a role in getting the American President to speak out against Sudan for the first time ever! But that Harvard event offered something even sweeter. My fellow students at the Boston Evening Academy had discovered that maybe I was not so stupid after all. Weeks later, when a new student wondered what the deal was with this tall, skinny African kid with the funny accent, I overheard one of my classmates say, "This guy, he's doing a big job."

School was still very difficult for me. My reading ability was far from perfect. My writing was not good. Someone advised me to try to write in the same way I talked and not to worry too much about grammar and punctuation. I tried it, and it did make writing less of a chore. But frankly, I was barely surviving. I was not sure if my English was improving. I had resisted English as Second Language courses, and there were none at the Boston Evening Academy. But Michelle Goldin came to my rescue again. She was so nice to me. "We know your story is different from most of the kids here," she said. "This is the first time we've had someone like you." She became my unofficial ESL teacher. Mr. Oliver, my adviser and humanities teacher, continued to work with me. And another teacher, Maggie Samp, also made sure I did my homework, and suggested that I might try working with some tutors over the summer to catch up in certain areas.

I worked hard and I tried hard. I think my teachers appreciated that. "Keep working hard," they said, and I listened to that advice. I worked on my English. When I didn't know a word, I looked it up in the dictionary and would write down the definition. Sometimes I would write down five or six definitions of the word. I kept lists of vocabulary words, which I studied. I read my schoolbooks with a dictionary. I listened to TV with a dictionary.

The first book I ever read on my own was *Kaffir Boy*, the autobiography of Mark Mathabane, the black South African writer. A teacher from another school located in the same building as Boston Evening Academy, who had heard me speak at Harvard, gave it to me. "It's a good book," he said. "He was feeling the same kinds of things you feel. He began to speak up and protest what was going on in South Africa." So I began reading *Kaffir Boy*, amazed that a country that once separated black Africans from white Africans could have changed so quickly. Mathabane writes about growing up in a shack in a black ghetto of Johannesburg under an apartheid system that he despised. It was a story that was familiar to me. He, too, wanted to escape the violence and racism of his childhood. Mathabane's "passport to freedom" was a scholarship to a small college in South Carolina in 1979. Living in the U.S., he began to wonder, if African-Americans had so recently demolished the racist idea that they were separate and unequal, and forced their nation to honor its commitment to democracy, why not the blacks in South Africa? He decided that he could work for social and political change in his country, not through violence but with words—as a journalist. As I made my way through *Kaffir Boy* with my dictionary, I kept thinking: If the South Africans could change so quickly, why not the Sudanese?

As hard as I worked at English in school, I really learned the language out on what Americans called "the lecture trail." By the end of 2001 and into the early months of 2002, in spite of my broken syntax and thin vocabulary, in spite of my heavy accent, I was speaking regularly at churches, synagogues, schools, and colleges. Thousands of people were hearing my story. In the beginning, I went with Charles, who would sit in the audience, taking pages of notes of words I misused, phrases I got wrong, and how I should vary the tone of my voice. After each speech we would go over his notes, and Charles would offer suggestions. Early on I had some serious problems with the English language. My vocabulary was limited, I got lost amidst various pronouns—I still sometimes say "she" when I mean "he"—and my grasp of verb tenses was slight. Often during a speech I would be aware that a sentence I had just said was probably garbled, but my audiences seemed to get my meaning. Other times I had no idea that I was speaking my own private version of English that no one could understand. For example, I would mix up "p" and "f," saying "fower" instead of "power" or "pood" when I meant "food." But with Charles coaching me, my speaking style gradually improved and my intense anxiety over standing in front of strangers lessened and eventually disappeared. Soon I was traveling by myself on trains and planes to cities up and down the East Coast and as far west as California—sometimes delivering more than ten speeches a month. Before each audience, I would apologize first for my terrible English, and then launch into my account of that day my mother sent me to the market with her eggs and beans with the older kids. I gave them the twenty-minute version of my story. Without notes. By the time of my Harvard appearance, I realized that I had already told my story so many times I didn't need to depend on a written speech. In fact, my ability to read was a lot less reliable than my memory, which had turned out to be very good. I had marveled at how Charles could stand up before an audience and give a speech without reading a word. Now I was doing the same thing: I just got up there and talked. I knew how the story began and how it ended. I was not about to forget what came in between. This was my story. It was my life.

And I not only managed to get the audiences to understand what I was saying, I was able to move them. In every audience, I could see people wiping away tears. Many expressed their outrage at both the governments of Sudan and the U.S. for allowing such horrors to continue in the world. My presentation worked. Giving so many speeches soon turned me into something of a professional performer, able to gauge my audiences, detecting the sympathetic people, and trying to win over the skeptics. By and large, the people who showed up were already interested or at least curious about the issue of slavery. Simply by telling what happened to me I could make an emotional connection with the audience. My feelings became their feelings. My passion became theirs.

In almost every audience I tell my story to someone asks me, "What kept you going?" I explain that my desire to see my parents again was strong. But I also stress to my audiences that I have always believed that without God's help I would have never made it. I always mention God in my speeches. I know God has been so important in my life. He kept me and delivered me. That's why I am here. Even though I don't read the Bible very often, I believe strongly in God. When you have something bad in your mind—in your life—that no one can help you with, you say, God, please help me with these things. When I faced this problem alone I had no one to talk with, no one to be friends with. I asked God to save me for a better time, to see my childhood friends again. Whenever I had a problem, I would appeal to God and ask Him to help me. And He encouraged me. I could feel it in my heart. I saw other Dinka kids who had lost their legs or who had gotten really sick. That never happened to me. I would pray to God to protect me. I look upon my survival, my escape from slavery, and my work on behalf of my people as proof that my prayers were heard. My most satisfying appearances were before school kids. After my speech to a Jewish elementary school in Newton, Massachusetts, a little boy got up during the question and answer period and said, "I do not have a question, I have a comment." I was amazed by his poise. He sounded like someone on the TV news, only a third as tall. He continued talking to me:

"People are always saying that movie stars and athletes are heroes. They are not heroes, they are *celebrities*. But you're a hero. You are my hero."

I will never forget that. What an amazing thing to say! I had given many speeches by then; after my trips to Washington, I began to realize that my work was effective. But I had never thought of myself as a "hero."

Not all of my listeners, however, have been so generous. Some people have not only resisted my message, they have been hostile to it and to me. My toughest moment came after a speech I gave at Penn State University that first year on the road. I had finished telling my story and asked if anyone had any questions. One guy raised his hand and stood up. He introduced himself and said he was from north Sudan and proceeded to read a statement in Arabic, which he translated to the audience.

"This is not a true story," he said. "There is no slavery in Sudan."

I stopped him and informed him that I was the one who had been invited to speak. I had asked for questions, not a political statement representing the Sudanese government. "You want to make another conflict," I said. "I'm here only to speak and tell a true story." Several other people stood up, also Arabs who maybe lived in the area, because they seemed to be older than the students. They claimed that the Dinka people had a wonderful life in the north. The violence was in the south, they said, and it was the result of "tribal conflict." Yes, there

were "abductions," but they were the result of one tribe stealing the children and animals of another tribe, something that
had been happening in the region for centuries.

"They are the ones who are lying," I told the audience,
explaining that it was only Muslims like them who were allowed
to have a wonderful life in Sudan. "How could they know about
what had happened to me?" I explained that I knew why they
had come to my speech, but I also knew why I had come to
America. Southern Sudanese were in conflict with northerners.
As northerners, they were defending their side, and I was
defending mine. But there was a difference: They were saying
what the government is saying, without considering that the
government might not be telling the truth. I had come to tell this
audience the truth about Sudan. This was a truth that I had discovered at the end of a gun and a whip. They, too, would have
to figure out the truth about Sudan on their own.

Then an American student stood up and told the audience
that this was not the first time he had heard about slavery in
Sudan. While he had never been to Sudan, he had read about
the issue of slavery in newspapers. "What he is saying is true,"
he told the other students. "And we need to listen to this."
Other students supported him and told the north Sudanese
that they had come to hear my side of the story.

I jumped back in and pointed out that I had been in Khartoum only a few years before and had seen people like them
living in big buildings in the city, shopping, eating in restaurants, their kids going to school, while my people lived in
refugee camps hours away where there was not even electricity
or proper water. Was that their idea of a "wonderful life"?
That seemed to silence them. And then something occurred to

me, and I could not resist sticking my hecklers with it: "I am also glad that you have shown up in front of all of these people," I said, "because you have given them a chance to see and listen to the kind of people I am talking about, the people enslaving my people, the kind of northern Sudanese who have put up with the murder of millions of Dinka."

Several more Arabs stood up and started arguing with me. I could tell that people in the audience were getting scared. But the students in charge of the meeting told the protestors that they had to let me finish my talk. When my time was up, my student hosts escorted me from the room and took me to my hotel. Apparently, soon after my speech was announced on campus, they had learned that local Arabs from Sudan disapproved of a southerner being allowed to speak. They were worried that things might get a bit hot, and when the argument broke out during the question period, they became concerned for my safety.

I have been interrupted so many times in my speeches, or attacked on the radio, that I have lost count. I have developed a way of handling my opponents, based on my replies to the north Sudanese who attacked me at Penn State: They are giving the government line, I am telling what I myself have witnessed and suffered. When they claim that I am not only anti-government (true) but that I am also against Islam (false), I point out that slavery in Sudan has been documented by international organizations, human rights groups, independent journalists. The United Nations and the U.S. government have confirmed the horrors that Sudan has brought upon the people of the south. I also stress that in northern Sudan they were told only what the government wanted them to know.

Here in America, a free country, I can tell my story, and I will keep on telling it. Sometimes I will remember to point out that one of the people crucial to my escape was the Muslim truck driver who took me from Mutari to ed-Da'ein, fed me, and housed me until he could afford to buy me a ticket to Khartoum. He was a good man. I am not an opponent of Islam.

Occasionally one of my critics will get very scary. At another speech, an Arab actually threatened me. "Be careful," he warned. "You are too young; you don't know enough about what has happened in Sudan."

"I know what I know," I informed him. "I may not be an expert on the history of Sudan, but I do know what I have been through, what I have witnessed." I told him to forget about politics. I was just telling my story.

Usually, when my critics see that I am not about to back down, that the audience is with me, it is they who sit down and shut up. I am not afraid to hit back with the moral force of my situation.

"I am not making this up," I assure my audiences. My body and mind bear the scars of the racism of the northern Sudanese people.

CHAPTER NINETEEN

WHY?

A line of questioning kept coming from my audiences: Why did this happen to you? How could those people do this to you? Why is there still slavery in the twenty-first century?

I told them only what I knew—about the endless war in Sudan between the Muslim Arabs of the north and the people of the south, many of them, like my parents, Christians, but most of them animists, devotees of traditional religions centered around the spirits of their ancestors. I explained that the Islamist government of the north wanted our cattle, our land, and the vast reserves of oil underneath it, but they wanted no part of us Dinka—except as cheap labor or slaves. Yes, Khartoum said that it wanted all Sudanese to be Muslims, but the Dinka boys who were forced to be educated as Muslims were also trained as soldiers and sent to the south to fight their own people. During most of the 1980s and '90s, Khartoum allowed military units and local militia groups near the border between the north and the south to raid the villages of the Dinka—and the Nuer and the Nuba—killing men, enslaving women and children, and turning villages into smoking huts. The survivors were forced to move north. According to international aid groups, two million southerners died and over four million more were displaced.

And the rest of the world ignored the horror of it all.

That's all that I knew. I had learned this much about why I had been enslaved and why my parents had been killed by talking to other Dinka in the camps in Khartoum, where most people were reluctant to talk for fear of government spies. But my real political education began in Cairo, where for the first time in our lives, we Dinka could talk about politics in our own land without fearing retaliation from Khartoum. There had been a long war, and the murahaliin did the government's killing and robbing to help themselves. Every Dinka I met in the camps and Cairo was a victim of this.

But as my audiences kept asking "why?" I realized I did not know enough to answer their questions adequately, even months after I had been working with the AASG. Well-informed college students, church members, and audiences at synagogues wanted to discuss the subtleties of Sudanese politics, holy war, why Islamist governments in Khartoum seem to be replaced by even more radical Islamist governments, the political splits inside the SPLA—the Sudanese People's Liberation Army, led by Dinka and Nuer rebels. And what about all that oil in the south? I did not have the answers. I apologized, confessing I had come only to tell them my story, to raise their consciousness about slavery in modern Sudan. The tragic story of my country was another matter that was still beyond me. After September 11, 2001, my audiences were even more interested—and better informed—about Islam and *jihad*.

I was determined to educate myself about Sudan. I wanted to be able to answer the questions after my speeches. I also wanted to be able to deal with my critics more forcefully. When northern Sudanese protested that what I was saying were "lies," that "there was no slavery in Sudan," I wanted to be able to demolish them with historical and political facts about their country—which was also my country. I also wanted to be able to make the connection between what was happening in Sudan and America's war on terror. I was eager to explain the similarities between the Taliban government in Afghanistan and the regime in Khartoum. I began to learn more about why my Dinka life had been taken from me. I talked to some of the experts, including some Dinka scholars living in the United States. As I studied more American and world history at the Boston Evening Academy, I also began to realize that what has happened in the past can often explain what is happening today. *Kaffir Boy* revealed to me that a black kid's experiences under apartheid in South Africa could help me understand the hatred and terrors of racism as well as the methods to wipe them out. I realized that another nation's success at dealing with racism might offer a road map to the future of Sudan. In one of my classes we were asked to read Charles Dickens's *A Tale of Two Cities*. For me, such a thick book was a daunting task. Like many of my fellow students, I wondered what relevance a story written more than a hundred years ago about the French Revolution—which had happened a hundred years before the book was published—had for our young lives in Boston.

Then I read the first sentence of *A Tale of Two Cities:* "It was the best of times, it was the worst of times."

I understood those words immediately. I had lived "the best of times" in Sudan as a child, but I had also known "the worst of times." My country had been in the worst of times for decades, and the rest of the world had to do something so that "the best of times" could return to Sudan. From my reading and study of history I have learned that every country goes through good and bad times. The U.S. had its own revolution, its own civil war, and fought in other foreign wars. But America's "best of times" outnumbers its troubled years. No matter how much people had told me about the wonders of America, I was in no way prepared for what this country has to offer refugees lucky enough to end up here. I was eager to know why some countries were so successful, while others, like my own, were such a catastrophe.

Above all, I had to learn why in my country Sudanese people murdered and enslaved other Sudanese people. That I was a slave for ten years I have told you. That my family was murdered is something I have only recently learned. I will now try to explain the reason why such terrible, unimaginable, and cruel things happened to me and my family—and millions of other south Sudanese people.[9]

Sudan is the largest nation in Africa, covering more than a million square miles. It stretches from the Red Sea in the East

---

[9] In addition to conversations with Charles Jacobs, Jesse Sage, and John Eibner, along with various reports of international human rights groups, two books by two Dinka scholars, men I am now honored to call friends, have helped educate me about my own people and country: *The Dinka of the Sudan* by Francis Mading Deng (Waveland Press, 1982) and Jok Maduk Jok's *War and Slavery in Sudan* (University of Pennsylvania Press, 2001). My account is an amateur's summary of Sudanese politics, mostly as it affected my tribe, the Dinka Malwal of West Aweil in southern Sudan. Anyone who wants to go deeper must read these books.

across the Nubian and Libyan Deserts, with Egypt and Libya to its north and the rain forests of Central Africa, Zaire, and Uganda in the south. The Dinka are Sudan's most numerous people, based across the Bahr al-Arab River that separates the north of Sudan from the south, where they have herded their cattle and farmed since the beginning of time and long before in the regions of the Upper Nile. Sudan is also the home of Africa's longest running war, which is usually described as a "civil war" between government forces and "rebel forces," now led by the Sudanese People's Liberation Army (SPLA). To be sure, south Sudanese military people did break away from the government. Yes, the battle has gone on for decades between the different peoples of the north and the south.

Yet, from what I can see, all this talk about "rebels" and "civil war" and "north versus south" has masked the underlying division between the two sides, which is as obvious as and deeper than the river dividing both sides, known as the Bahr al-Arab to the Arabs and Kiir to the Dinka. Africa's longest running war would not exist if there were not centuries of racism north of the river and almost twenty years of religious arrogance and cruelty. That was not always the easiest argument to make in America— at least before September 11, 2001. While what the Taliban did to the people of Afghanistan may have seemed strange to you in the West, to us southern Sudanese, the terror and cruelty of such an extreme form of Islam is as familiar as our homes of wood, mud, and straw, which our enemies enjoyed setting aflame, too often with women and children inside. And while Osama bin Laden strikes most Americans as a crazy terrorist from Saudi Arabia, we Sudanese remember that before he went to Afghanistan he lived in Sudan, protected by the equally fanatical

Islamist government that remains in power. Imagine a country filled with Osama bin Ladens, and then imagine those views—a radical Islam in a constant jihad against the Christian and animist "infidels" within their own country—being official government policy. As unreal as that might strike Americans, it has been the reality of Dinka life for decades.

From my studies I have concluded that what happened to me was about racism and religion—mainly about religion. Since 1983, various governments in Khartoum have made it the law that the Sudanese can practice only one religion, their brand of Islam. Anyone who resists, even Muslims, are branded "infidels" and become fair game in Khartoum's jihad, their "holy war" to create an ideal Islamic state—the same kind of fundamentalist urge that has created turmoil in Pakistan, Indonesia, and Afghanistan under the late and unlamented Taliban. Politics causes wars, and throughout history it has done so: defending the nation's security, acquiring more territory, therefore more security. But enslaving little African boys, killing two million southerners and running more than four million out of their homes and villages—that kind of savagery takes more than mere politics; it takes a pure ideological commitment, a kind of irrational fanaticism, and nothing seems to be able to fuel that kind of radical commitment better than religion. When you add religious fanaticism to an ancient feeling of superiority of one people to another, you have a deadly and extremely cruel combination—as Americans found out on September 11.

"There come the camels!" That has been a cry of fear among the Dinka of Sudan for centuries. I was amazed to find out that even before Muhammad originated his religion and established the first Islamic state in the seventh century, Arabs had been raiding villages in southern Sudan and taking women and children as their slaves. For centuries, the two peoples kept their distance. Yet, even under the rule of the Turks and Egyptians slavery was still permitted. For the Muslims of the area that would become Sudan, the Dinka were only fit to be slaves, and thus their word for "black people" and "slaves" became the same: abeed.

The modern state of Sudan was an invention of the British, who defeated the Ottoman Empire and rearranged its peoples into various national, tribal, and mixed states throughout the Middle East and Africa. Too often they created nations already divided by ethnic animosities, making civil war inevitable, and Sudan is a notorious case in point: Suddenly the Dinka of southern Sudan and the Arabs of the north, wary allies in the best of times, found themselves as citizens in the same nation. Neither side could forget the slave raids of the past, and the British did their best—for strategic rather than humanitarian reasons—to keep the north and south geographically divided and culturally distinct. The colonial rulers initiated a "Southern Policy" that discouraged cultural contacts or assimilation between northerners and southerners and allowed Christian missionaries into the south. The pride of the Dinka was legendary, even among the Europeans. My people believed that they already lived in heaven and that Dinka who went to live in the north or any place else were crazy. Historically, the Dinka have been a people who preferred peace, but when their way of life was threatened, or their precious cattle were stolen, they would fight back. The colonial government saw such independence and tribal pride as a threat.

The British did not know quite what to do with the peoples of southern Sudan. "The more they stayed in the abyss of backwardness the better," a historian of the Dinka, Francis Mading Deng, has written of the British attitudes toward the tribes of the south. The son of a famous "Paramount Chief" of the Ngok Dinka, Deng was educated in the north where he also taught law and then earned graduate degrees in law at Yale in the 1960s before working for the UN's Human Rights Division. He also taught law at New York University and Columbia. In the 1970s, Deng was Sudan's foreign minister as well as its ambassador to Canada and the United States. In his book, *The Dinka*, he explains that "The notion of the 'Noble Savage' added to the policy of preservation. Although some Southern tribes were judged harmless and were receiving more modern benefits than others, the whole south remained a museum of nature." For the British, according to Ambassador Deng, the political future of the south "ranged from affiliation with Uganda to total independence." A united Sudan was not in the cards.

But neither was a future for Britain in Africa and the Middle East. After World War II, the policy of a separate north and south was abandoned. The British still stayed close to Khartoum, while the Dinka and the Arabs discovered the shared goal of getting rid of the colonials. Meantime, their large neighbor to the north, Egypt, was also shedding British colonialism and had an eye on Sudan. Soon, however, the British were gone, transferring power to the northerners. In January 1956 "The Republic of Sudan" emerged as an independent state, with the northerners still believing that they could ignore the south, which pushed for a federal system that would give the non-Muslims of Sudan a voice in government. That issue is still on the table. Civil war intervened.

Even before independence, a group of southern soldiers

mutinied, sparking a civil war that would last for sixteen years. The Dinka, according to Deng, saw military revolt as "premature" and continued to work for a federation. But efforts to convert the south to Islam and Arabize the culture continued, and "governments changed, democracy came and went," notes Deng. "It was no longer possible for the southerner to be heard." The Dinka finally joined the rebels. And so my people, who since the beginning of memory had viewed their lives and homeland as a kind of heaven on earth filled with valuable cattle and farmland, found themselves singing sad songs about "the feud, the feud, the feud of the southerners and northerners; our feud will never end." For the next sixteen years the fighting continued, and so did the efforts of the north to Arabize the south, which only persuaded the southerners—who had lost 500,000 people in the fighting—that they might never be able to live in the same country with people who cared nothing for their cultures and religions. But these same cultural and language differences—experts point to as many as six hundred ethnic groups in the south speaking some four hundred languages—turned into a political liability. It was easy for Khartoum to instigate hostilities between local tribes in the south, thus undercutting any chance of a united front against the north. The largest ethnic group of the south was the Dinka, and hundreds of thousands of them sought refuge in neighboring African countries.

The first round of the civil war ended in 1972 with an agreement that gave the south its own legislature and control over its natural resources—which, much to Khartoum's dismay, were soon discovered to include oil. In 1983, General Ja'far Nimeiri, who had taken power in a military coup in 1969, canceled the agreement, stripped the southern legislature of its power, and announced that the oil from the south would be refined in the north. Worse still, Nimeiri, who had become a devout and extreme Muslim, instituted Islamic *shariah* law throughout the entire nation, subjecting even Christians and animists to such traditional cruel punishments as being stoned to death or having an arm chopped off for the crimes of adultery or drinking.

Once again, southern army officers who, according to the terms of the 1972 treaty, were supposed to stay in the south, refused government orders to move north, bridled at Khartoum's power play and mutinied. Khartoum sent the Dinka officer John Garang, then head of the Sudan Military Research Bureau in the capital, to mediate the dispute—unaware that Garang was part of the conspiracy he was sent to defuse. The government sent fifteen thousand troops to put down the mutiny, but the rebels withdrew into the bush. Six months later the Sudanese People's Liberation Army was born under the leadership of Colonel Garang. The result was round two of the civil war.

This was the Sudan of my childhood, the war-and-famine-ravaged south that my father traveled around for business, though my parents seemed to have insulated us from the bad news that they surely could not have ignored. I recall occasionally hearing neighbors and village people talking of "war;" references to the murahaliin were so common that the significance of these Arabs with guns was lost on a little Dinka boy whose main concern was how he and his playmates would fill up the day. But, while my family seemed well off, many people in the village were poor and hungry, and now I have a better idea of why. From my reading, I learned that Dinka relations with the cattle-herding Arab tribes directly north of us—the

people known as the "Baggara Arabs"[10] that included Giemma
and his Rizeigat neighbors—disintegrated quickly. In his book,
Jok Madut Jok points out that drought hit the Baggara
provinces of Darfu and Kordofan, and the Arabs brought their
cattle across the Kiir to graze in the grasslands of the Dinka.
My people tried to keep them out of their land, but the Baggara began showing up armed and willing to force their way
southward. People got killed on both sides. Such Arab-Dinka
clashes had happened off and on for generations; they were
about cattle and grass, not politics and religion. The government could have kept things under control. Instead, Khartoum
decided to ignore the illegal accumulation of arms among the
Baggara and use the cattle herders as allies in their own efforts
to regain control of the south.

As hostilities escalated in the Dinka grazing areas, the SPLA
stationed troops along the Kiir, reestablishing the British colonial
government's border between the north and south and driving
off any Baggara who tried to move into the Dinka pastures. The
rebel forces also moved against the Sudanese army and into non-
Arab areas across the border in the Nuba Mountains and the
Ingressana hills of the southern Blue Nile, the home of other
African tribes. Suddenly something historic happened. Tradition-
ally, the Nuba and Ingressana people (along with the Beja of eastern Sudan and the Fur of the west) had been the prime recruits
for the army of Sudan, fighting under Arab officers, of course.
Also suffering under Arab and Muslim arrogance, young men
and women of these African Muslim tribes began joining the

---

[10] Like the Dinka, these Muslims were cattle people. The Arabic word for
cattle is "baggara."

SPLA. According to Jok Madut Jok, "Such unity among non-Arabs of Sudan, which had never happened before, sent a wave of fear through the Arab and Muslim rulers in Khartoum."

The rebels gradually became a more formidable fighting force and Garang was broadcasting reports via SPLA Radio across Sudan, charging that Nimeiri's government was manipulating racism and tribal conflicts to rob the nation. The war was also costing a reported million dollars a day, and Nimeiri's grasp on power was loosening. In April 1985, Nimeiri was finally booted out of power by a popular uprising supported by the army—*while he was visiting Washington trying to persuade the U.S. to continue its military support against the southern rebels.*

This fact amazed me. I had no idea that the Americans had supported Khartoum against the south and that troops fighting against the SPLA were using guns as well as fighter jets and transport planes from the U.S. But reports of human rights abuses by Khartoum were flowing into Washington, and the U.S. began pulling back its support. Nimeiri went to the U.S. to make his case. While he was out of the country, his enemies took the opportunity to replace him with a "transitional" military regime that promised to prepare for elections for a civilian government and asked the SPLA to join elections, now that the dictator had been removed. But Garang balked, and watched as Sadiq al-Mahdi was elected prime minister, leading a coalition of parties that had been in and out of power in previous elected governments since independence. Mahdi resisted repealing Nimeiri's oppressive Islamic laws, the same ones that he had vigorously criticized in his opposition to the previous regime. Mahdi also went out of his way to attack Garang as being "influenced by foreign sources to preach hate against the

Arabs and Muslims." Mahdi continued Nimeiri's policy of dealing with the south only with guns.

Khartoum needed more soldiers for the war against the south. With its traditional reserves of Nuba and other African army recruits joining the SPLA, the Mahdi government looked to the Baggara Arabs and was not disappointed. It was a perfect opportunity for the Baggara herders to pursue age-old economic goals in Dinkaland under the guise of governmental supporters. Armed Baggara tribes formed their own militia groups—the infamous murahaliin. Excited by Khartoum's declaration of jihad against the south, students and other civilians rushed to arms, joined by adults forced to spend six weeks of compulsory military training, working with army units and the murahaliin. This paramilitary group became known as the "Popular Defense Forces" (PDF). Supplied with weapons, money, army insignia, and pumped up with the religious belief that the SPLA was an enemy of Islam, PDF members also called themselves *mujahideen*, holy warriors. These forces routinely accompanied government trains through the south to guard them against SPLA attacks, the Baggara militias on horseback and on foot guarding the outer perimeter along the tracks. As they passed Dinka villages, the militia would make a quick attack, taking cattle and slaves. Jok's research in the area indicated that moving slaves to the north was mainly left to the militias, but there was also evidence that regular army soldiers as well as PDF fighters would grab Dinka children and bring them back to their barracks or even villages when they went on leave, claiming to have rescued the kids from war. Many of those kids reportedly were sent to Islamic schools and were brainwashed into future holy warriors used to fight against their own people.

According to Jok, "the first and most destructive attack on the
Dinka communities of Aweil, Abyei, and Tuic occurred in February 1986." Over the next few months, Rizeigat militias
attacked and looted Malwal Dinka villages of Aweil on an
almost daily basis and, according to Jok, "took two thousand
women and children and thousands of cattle."

I was one of those children. At the time, of course, I had no
idea of the extent of the militia attacks or the numbers of victims. But according to books and various reports from human
rights organizations, during this second round of civil war,
which is still technically under way, two million southerners
have died from the fighting or the famine and disease caused
by the war; 4.4 million more have been forced from their
homes and villages, many to the north where they hoped the
government would protect them. (In the U.S. Civil War, which
lasted four years, 620,000 Americans were killed.) After the
SPLA set up its base across the border in the Nuba Mountains,
the government used this as an excuse to hammer the Nuba,
killing some one hundred thousand and creating a million
homeless Nuba refugees. Hunger is always a problem during
war, but in 1988 a drought decreased already meager food supplies and 250,000 people reportedly died.

The economy only got worse, but the attacks on the south,
particularly the murahaliin raids, were encouraged in hopes that
the fighting and misery would destabilize the south and turn the
people against the SPLA. But the southern rebels kept fighting
back. Efforts to bring peace were opposed by the Islamic hard-
liners, who feared the return of a secular state. In 1989, a group
of military officers staged another coup that not only ended

al-Mahdi's rule but, backed by the hard-line National Islamic Front, abolished the existing constitution, outlawed all political opposition, and replaced the National Assembly with the "Revolutionary Command Council for National Salvation," which proceeded to purge the army and step up the war against the south. The Revolutionary Council was soon replaced by a civilian government whose main goal was to establish a radical "Islamic State." The government declared jihad against Christians in the south and any other religious groups who were not Muslims. Anyone opposed to government policies, according to international human rights groups, risked arrest, torture, and execution. Khartoum also gave the Baggara license to kill, rob, and enslave these enemies and settle their lands.

And thus, between 1983 to the end of the century, through several regimes in Khartoum, the Arabs continued their trips into the south for traditional slave raiding and cattle robbery, not only with government support but also the added justification that they were playing an essential role in Khartoum's jihad against non-Muslims in Sudan. They attacked villages of the south with the kind of ferocity and cruelty that only religion can inspire, enslaving and killing people like me and my family as if we were not human. I was amazed to read a story that Jesse showed me in *The New Yorker* magazine about "The Invisible War" in Sudan. The reporter visited the Aweil area and then the marketplace from which I had been snatched. This statement was particularly astonishing to me: "Nyamlell has been suffering seasonal raids by the Rizeigat and the Misseriya [another Baggara Arab group] for fifteen years, and the SPLA's defense of the area has been mostly ineffective, but the local

Dinka have refused to abandon their lands. This year, however, they got hit harder than ever."[11]

That was 1998! Twelve years after the raid I had seen with my own eyes, Arabs had raided Nyamlell, according to this article, four times that year alone—on horseback, on camels, on donkeys, on foot, in Toyota pickups, shooting with machine guns. "It was the Army and the PDF and the murahaliin, all together," said a village magistrate named Martin Mawiens Dut, an educated Dinka who spoke English. "They conquered the town, burning it down, taking slaves for six or seven days." The raiders chopped down mango trees and broke the clay pots the locals used for water. They also collected as many goats and cattle and people as they could find and moved them all north. Among the people were Martin Dut's wife and five-year-old son.

I was an ex-slave, already in Cairo going through the refugee process, and the murahaliin were still stealing little boys from the market town of Nyamlell. The reporter noticed that young men in Nyamlell were scarce. Over the years the raiders had stolen millions of cattle, depriving the people of their wealth and the center of their culture. Without cattle, there could be no "bridewealth"—the cattle paid to the wife's family—and without marriage there would be fewer Dinka children to replace the men who had been killed and the women and children who had been taken away to the north.

To me this cultural damage was almost more upsetting than the violence to people. I had experienced the cruelty of dislocation and slavery. But one of the things that helped me survive

---

[11] "The Invisible War," William Finnegan, *The New Yorker*, January 25, 1999.

was the dream of one day returning home. The more I read and learn about what has happened to my people during the time I have been away makes me wonder what will be left of the Dinka life by the time I am able to return to Sudan. I thought I had escaped the violence of the north Sudanese. But because of the devastating effects of the raids and the war on my people, Sudan's violence seems to be able to reach me even in America. The war in Sudan may be "invisible" to Americans and others in the world, but to us south Sudanese it is a constant and painful presence.

I know that not all Sudanese Muslims approve of their government's policies. I owe my life to that truck driver from ed-Da'ein who believed that taking slaves was against his religion. But how do the rest justify enslaving me and so many others?

Many deal with the issue of slavery in Sudan by saying exactly what my Arab hecklers say to my face (and to my audiences): "There is no slavery in Sudan!" The Dinka have been driven by the war and famine northward. They are poor and jobless, and who else would be doing the menial jobs in the north? Yes, there are Dinka people who do work in the north and who might even be paid; some might also be willing to work for food and shelter.

I did neither. For, while Giemma fed me and housed me, he did so to keep me strong enough for working and not as compensation for taking care of his cattle. I worked for this family for ten years without any choice, and that is a big difference. I did not turn up at his house for a handout. I was carried there against my will, forced to work, and the few times I complained

I was beaten severely. And what about those warnings that those who complained got their arms or legs chopped off? And what about that day I was caught escaping and Giemma told me, "This is your last night on earth"? I was not just some "guest worker" in northern Sudan for ten years. I was a slave who worked for no pay with both a whip and the threat of death hanging over me every single day I decided to do otherwise. If I was not a slave, then Giemma Abdullah owes me a pile of Sudanese pounds for ten years' hard labor.

And what about the raids? Jok Madut Jok quotes an explanation from one Baggara Arab: "Our raids have nothing do with slavery; we want cattle, we want the Dinka grazing land; if they stand in the way, capturing is the way to frighten them." So is shooting the men and chopping them down in the marketplace of Nyamlell. I will never forget what I saw: the murahaliin swinging their swords at Dinka, as if a sword could not cut a living man. That scares people, all right. And so does carrying off their children and forcing their wives to work and have sex. I find it hard to believe anyone whose people have been enslaving Dinkas for more than a thousand years who claims that slavery is the furthest thing from their minds. These are, after all, the same people for whom the word "abeed" covers black people, slaves, or filth. Who would trust them not to take slaves? To be sure, some Arabs have been known to release Dinka no longer useful to them. And not all the Dinka are used for work. Many young boys are brainwashed into Muslim life, trained to fight with the militia, and forced to join in raids on the villages of their own people.

"It's because of the war" is another common explanation for the slave raids, maybe the most common. The SPLA is

largely Dinka, led by Dinka, and therefore is supported by
Dinka. Do the rebels of the south, one argument goes, think that
they can attack government forces without retaliation? My
father was not an SPLA fighter, and while there may have been
some rebels around that marketplace, the women and children
taken away were not in the SPLA. Are not wars supposed to distinguish between warriors and innocent civilians, especially
women and children? History also counters this explanation for
the murahaliin raids as being merely local acts of retaliation in a
civil war. For generations the same cattle-herding Arabs who
make up the militias have not required a government-sanctioned
war to kill Dinka or to steal their cattle or women and children.
In fact, after 1983, increasingly radical Islamist governments
encouraged them to kill and exploit innocent civilians by turning
the civil war into a "holy war" whose primary aim was to dominate the south and plunder its economic resources. Proof of
that aim came when southern Muslims—the Nuba people, for
example—who opposed this new extreme form of Islamic State
were declared "infidels" and became targets of the same holy
war that was ravaging tribes where people followed Christianity
and their traditional religions. And few benefited more from this
policy than the Baggara Arabs, who could pursue their age-old
goal of annexing the Dinka cattle and grasslands and justify it as
their patriotic as well as religious duty.

The Dinka know that their Arab neighbors to the north
have nothing but contempt for them—that they are perceived
only as an obstacle to having more cattle and better grasslands.
And the Baggara Arabs have not tried to keep their distaste for
us southerners a secret. From everything I can read, and from
what the international human rights experts say, the Arabs of

northern Sudan look upon Dinka and the other African tribes of the south as peoples born to be slaves—abeed.

Imagine what a revelation this was to me! The first Arabic word my seven-year-old ears had ever distinguished from the song Giemma's kids sang as they beat me with sticks was abeed. I soon learned that this was the northern Sudanese word for a south Sudanese. It was the same word they used for everyone below them socially and economically—poor people were abeed, and that usually meant south Sudanese African people. But they used the same word to denote a dirty, filthy person even of their own race. Abeed, in fact, is one of the most obscene words in their language, and they applied it to me and my people without a thought. Jok Madut Jok explains this clearly, and he also says something that sums up my own experience so well:

I do not want to reduce the tragic experience of slavery to the mere use of a word, but the Arab notion that Southerners are people who are naturally slaves goes beyond demeaning terms. Even if one were to make an argument that Sudanese slavery is a product of war, the war itself is result of degrading views that Northerners hold of Southerners, and these views are responsible for slavery.

This was certainly my experience. Giemma justified his cruelty to me by calling me "an animal." I thought this excuse was just Giemma's craziness. I had no idea that the animal status of the Dinka was the predominant opinion of his half of Sudan.

Yet this feeling that the other side is not human, I have

learned, has never been mutual. For as much as the Dinka have come to hate those Baggara Arabs who have turned our lives into hell, as much as the Dinka prefer their own culture to that of the Muslims, I have never heard any of my people claim that we are superior to the Arabs. Jok makes this point in his book, and my own experience bears it out. Even when I first came to America and people asked me about what shocked me most about my life in the North apart from the cruelty, I always answered, "Our cultures are so different, the food was different; we have different religions." And as I write this, I am reminded that when I saw my first Arabs in the marketplace one day, my father explained that these men were Sudanese from the North, who had a different religion and a different way of life from ours in the South.

The Dinka have gone out of their way to help the Arabs, even during the war. I was surprised to read in Jok's book that there were truces between the Dinka and the Baggara during the time I was living with Giemma. In 1989, the International Committee of the Red Cross was vaccinating Dinka cattle against a disease that was infecting cattle on both sides of the border, while the Baggara were depending on Khartoum, whose veterinary services were not coming through. Fearing that the Arab cows were likely to reinfect the Dinka herds that sometimes met in the grazing valleys of the Kiir River ("Bahr al-Arab" to the Arabs), the Dinka invited the Baggara to join their vaccinations. After the vaccination process, in gratitude, according to Jok, "instead of returning peacefully, they attacked Dinka villages and cattle camps and the truce broke down."

A year later, according to Jok, my people allowed the Baggara to enter Dinka territory once again to trade at three major Dinka markets for the dry season, and when their time was up "they killed people, took slaves, and burned the markets to the ground." Yet the Dinka proceeded to renew both peace agreements for the next eight years, until they finally realized that such a one-sided truce brought them only bloodshed and thievery. Khartoum sent government agents along with the Baggara traders to spy on the SPLA and to pick fights in the marketplace that erupted into Dinka-Baggara brawls. No sooner had the Dinka expelled the Arabs for breaking the peace than they were back raiding villages. "They do not keep their word," the Dinka commissioner of Awiel West told Jok in a 1999 interview in Nyamlell. "They are being used against us by the government; so, until they come to their senses about our common good, we will cooperate no more."

They do not respect us. For the past two decades, who was running Sudan did not matter for my people. The policies were essentially the same: more civil war, new militia raids, murder, famine, forced Islamization, millions of people fleeing north, where Dinka boys were kidnapped by the army, trained and sent back to the south to fight the SPLA. It did not matter how hard the Dinka tried to win that respect. Why would they respect us when a thousand years of racism and religious belief had taught them to consider us Dinka to be inferior human beings, natural slaves—abeed.

Another argument made against the existence of slavery is, "Show us the documentation of slavery." Of course, those who make this point do not mention that the Sudanese government has banned human rights organizations from investigating charges of slavery in their country. Any Sudanese who even raises the issue risks imprisonment or worse, as I myself discovered in Khartoum. For decades, there had not been much proof from international organizations of the government backing slave taking or trafficking in Sudan. There have never been any slave revolts because slaves are not allowed to spend enough time with each other to organize. I have read about American slavery, groups of people working in the fields, their music and prayers in the slave quarters, with a strange sense of envy. If only I had men and women and other children to be with at night!—instead of the dreary loneliness of my ten years, where to talk to another Dinka in our native language was to risk a beating or losing a limb.

The Dinka know about the slave raids; the facts are part of almost all our lives. But ours is an oral tradition. My people told stories about the raids and slaves—they sang about slavery. But they did not write books or newspaper stories about their suffering. And they certainly did not file reports to international human rights organizations. That is changing, as Dinka refugees move to the West and organize. In 1992, Britain's House of Lords addressed the issue of slavery in Sudan; two years later, there were conferences in Bonn and London about the issue. By the mid-1990s independent investigators began producing evidence of slavery and other human rights abuses in Sudan. Groups such as Africa Watch, Amnesty International, and the Sudanese Human Rights Organization have also documented abuses in Sudan.[12] In 1996, a columnist for

---

[12] Allison Wiebalck, "Slavery in Sudan: a challenge to international law," *The Comparative and International Law Journal of Southern Africa*, XXXI (1998), pp. 38–60. The American Anti-Slavery Group keeps track of the reports from the human rights community and other news on slavery in Sudan and other countries. For the existing documentary evidence, see the AASG Web site iAbolish.com.

the *Times* of London called the Sudan regime "a slave state of our time."[13] Special United Nations investigators have confirmed slavery in Sudan, as well as the government's role in supporting the slave raiders.

And if "there are no slaves," who are those women and children that John Eibner's Christian Solidarity International is redeeming from the north—for the price of two Sudanese goats? a person? Asked in 1995 by Dinka leaders to help with redeeming slaves in Sudan, CSI, as I write, has helped gain the release of more than 80,000 people. These redemptions are controversial, even among human rights groups. Critics charge that paying money for slaves will only encourage Baggara Arabs to abduct more people in order to sell them to CSI. United Nations International Children's Emergency Fund (UNICEF) has attacked the redemptions as "absolutely intolerable." And the 2002 U.S.-led international commission that confirmed the existence of slavery in Sudan also questioned whether slave redemptions were helping the situation. John Eibner has argued that there is no hard evidence that his work has increased the market in slaves, while there is proof in the smiling faces of those liberated that redemptions have saved many lives and improved the lives of thousands more.

Frankly, I wish money did not have to change hands. I also would prefer that the struggle for peace and liberation in Sudan be beyond any criticism. Charles insists that I am wrong: The lives—and futures—of the liberated slaves are worth the criticism and certainly the price, which has remained

---

[13] Bernard Levin, *Times* of London, May 31, 1996.

consistent and relatively low. Charles says that the cost of fifty to seventy dollars a slave, the current equivalent of the market price for two goats, proves that the Baggara aren't doing it only for the money and how little they value Dinka people—so little that they are unable to imagine an international group paying more money per head.) But Charles and I can agree that arguing over redemption tends to divert attention and energy from the real moral issue: slavery in Sudan. Even UN and U.S. critics of the practice of redeeming slaves for money concede that slavery exists in Sudan. Based on raid patterns over the past fifteen or so years, and the observations of travelers, CSI has estimated a total of some 100,000 "chattel slaves" being held across the border in the Darfur and Kordofan areas of Sudan—not even counting the boys forced to attend religious schools where they are trained as holy warriors against their own people.[14]

In 2000, Susan Rice, the assistant secretary of state for African affairs whom I met in Washington, went to Sudan to see for herself the effects of Khartoum's human rights abuses. President Bill Clinton put her outrage into words by attacking "the scourge of slavery in Sudan." (After she left office, Rice wrote an opinion piece in the *Washington Post* about talking to civilians wounded in the aerial bombing of their villages by government forces.) In 2001, Colin Powell, a new secretary of state in a new administration, told a congressional hearing on legislation to get the U.S. to intervene in Sudan, "There is perhaps no greater tragedy on the face of the earth today than the tragedy that is unfolding in Sudan."

---

[14] John Eibner has documented CSI's work in "My Career Redeeming Slaves," Middle East Quarterly, December, 1999.

Yet the United Nations—that same institution that heard my
story and gave me refugee status and the opportunity to go to
the U.S.—has been alarmingly silent on the issue. The UN Secretary General Kofi Annan has never publicly condemned
Sudan's role in the slave trade. Only when CBS News did a
story on Sudanese slaves and CSI's work did UNICEF admit
for the first time publicly that "Slavery in Sudan exists."[15] That
as recently as 2001 a Dinka scholar named Jok Madut Jok,
who teaches at Loyola Marymount University in Los Angeles,
must publish a book called *War and Slavery in Sudan* to make the
case that Sudanese slavery does exist is quite astonishing to
someone like me whose life is evidence of what has been going
on for so long.

So, here is my own attempt to offer documentation of the
existence of slavery in Sudan: my life, my story, this book.

---

[15] Eibner, Middle East Quarterly, December 1999.

CHAPTER TWENTY

FINALLY, SOME GOOD
NEWS FROM SUDAN

Charles treated me like a son. "How are you doing, Francis?" he would ask me. "What do you need?" Whenever I had a question or needed advice, I went to Charles and he was ready to help. "We want you to be the person you want to be, Francis. I'm here to help you with anything."

And he did. As independent as I tried to be, much of American life was still a mystery to me, and Charles did his best to help me get comfortable in Boston while I was working with the AASG. He made sure I had a place to live and was paid for my work. He helped me get to school. I could call him at any time of the day or night with a problem (and I often did) and he would help me fix it. One look into my eyes and Charles knew whether I was happy or not. Above all, through his connections and friends he got my story out. He showed me how powerful one person's story could be, and in that way he proved to me how powerful I could be.

"You're making a difference for your people," he kept telling me, and I kept working harder to prove him right. Charles watched over my new life in Boston. For four months or so I lived with his neighbors, the Bales. Charles had also introduced me to Roxbury Baptist Church and its inspirational pastor, Gerald Bell. Ever since I gave my first speech there, I was drawn back to Roxbury Baptist on Sundays to a community of black faces who recognized me, who smiled and shook my hand, who were happy to see me. Pastor Bell reached out to me and helped me deal with the death of my parents. Occasionally he dropped by at the Bales's to talk and play a little basketball with me in the driveway, where there was a hoop on the garage. This was a very nice man, obviously intelligent and successful, with a busy church to run, boards to sit on, yet still willing to spend time with a lonely and not-so-articulate teenager from Africa trying to settle into another strange city in a country that was truly incredible to him. He and his wife Cynthia invited me to their house for dinner with them and their two children. When someone mentioned "Christian charity," I now knew exactly what they were talking about. Even when I moved into my Boston apartment, Pastor Bell would drive into the city, pick me up, and drive me to his service. But I was used to having my own place, and Charles found me a studio apartment in a building in downtown Boston, near Fenway Park. I was the only one in the building who was not American. In the summer, students working or studying in Boston would move in. The noise was annoying, but not as much as the one thousand dollars a month I was paying for the pleasure of the constant sound of loud music, parties, and my own loneliness. Ames had spoiled me. I needed to be surrounded by more people like me. I was back in touch with Franco, who lived with his wife and children in Lynn, a working-class town north of the airport where many Dinka now lived. I asked him to find me a place nearby, and soon he told me about a woman he knew who might be moving to New Hampshire and giving up a two-bedroom apartment in his neighborhood. I met with her and found out that she would not be leaving for a couple of months. But she introduced me to the landlord and said that I wanted to take over the apartment when she moved. He agreed—if I would put down a small deposit and be willing to pay fifty dollars more a month for rent, which would be seven hundred dollars. It was a deal, especially to be near the growing Dinka community in Lynn, where the famous African-American former slave and abolitionist Frederick Douglass wrote his life story. The only drawbacks: I would have a 30-minute-or-more commute by bus and subway to the AASG offices in downtown Boston; going to church in Roxbury would also be impossible.

When I moved in I bought a TV and a stereo. I also got a computer and set up the second bedroom as an office where I could do my homework and keep in touch on-line with the AASG. My speaking engagements had increased, and Charles made sure that I got the fees. I was also getting a decent monthly income from the AASG. And it wasn't long before I discovered that, while my English was still shaky and much of American food still did not appeal to me, one American habit came to me very naturally: shopping. I seemed to have a pair of sneakers for every occasion. But looking good and buying fine things made me happy, and I had suffered too long in my short life to miss opportunities to make myself feel good.

Occasionally, I was too good to myself, spending my pay so quickly that when the bills came in I didn't have enough money to pay them. "I'm in trouble," I would say to Charles. He would advance me some money, but he also gave me a warning: "You must pay your bills on time. And don't spend your money so carelessly."

Only your parents would tell you such important things. Only people who cared about you a lot would worry that way. I remember needing to talk to him about some problem I was having, and I walked into his office. The door is always open, but this day Charles was on the phone. As soon as he saw me (and probably caught a troubled look in my eye) he said into the phone, "I'll call you back." He then hung up and asked me what was wrong. I am sure there are times that I drive poor Charles crazy. "How are you doing with your money, Francis?" he will ask, just at the time when I am not doing so well with my money. He always tries to help, just like any parent would. One thing that I noticed immediately about Charles was that he had no need to play "the important person." In my travels I had come across many men who needed to be in charge. Charles was my boss, the founder and president of an important group, a man who had been awarded a prize for his work by Coretta Scott King and who could get congressmen on the phone in Washington. But he never once ordered me around or even asked me to get him a cup of coffee or a glass of water. During that first year when Charles and I were traveling together to my speaking engagement, I would try to help him with his bags. He always insisted on handling them by himself.

Sitting on the plane or a train together during those early months, I learned about his life and family. The more he told me, the more I admired Charles and the luckier I felt to have met him. He had his family and his own business. His life was comfortable, but one day Charles read someplace that you could still buy a slave in Sudan, and he stopped working and plowed his savings into starting an organization to fight slavery. "Why?" I asked him. His answer was simple: "What good is life, Francis, if you can't help other people, if you can't fix things? And how can you not act when there is slavery?" We Dinka are blessed that someone like Charles Jacobs turned his whole life toward trying to fix Sudan, and I will make sure the south Sudanese people will never forget what he has done.

When I found out that my parents had been killed, Charles was worried about me. He wondered whether I should talk to a psychologist. I suspect he thought that maybe I was holding too much inside me, that I had been through too much, and the bad news about my family might injure me for good. I did not want any help. I wanted to deal with this latest misery in the way that I dealt with all those that had come before it. Long ago in my little hut near the goats on Giemma's farm, I learned how a dream could blot out pain and loss. Many people have asked me how I felt when I finally learned that I would never see my parents again. I was devastated, of course. That phone call hurt more than the worst beating I ever got from Giemma. The pain of his whip always went away. I will never stop missing my parents.

But they are dead, and I cannot do anything about that. It will not do me—or them—any good, no matter how long I might sit with a psychologist. I have dealt with a lot in my life, and I am dealing with my parents' death in much the same way: I am thinking about the future and praying for God's continued help. My parents had great hopes for me, and I have decided that the best way to honor their memory is to try to achieve great things for our people.

My life has also taught me that, even during "the worst of

times," one day the phone can ring, and there can be another miracle at the other end.

One morning, I woke up to find a message on my cell phone. When I checked, I heard John Eibner's voice. He was calling from a satellite phone in southern Sudan, in the East Aweil area, in fact, and he wanted me to talk to someone. Suddenly, I heard a strange voice speaking Dinka.

"Piol," he said, using my Dinka name. "This is your brother Buk Bol Buk. I'm here with your friends, the group you work with, and we will call you again tomorrow." And he hung up.

I replayed the message. His voice was very different from the one I still held in my memory. But that was thirteen years before, which meant that my big brother was now over thirty years old. He would speak with the voice of a grown man. I couldn't believe he was calling me. I still couldn't believe he was alive. My family had not been wiped out after all. I still had a brother.

Ever since I heard that my parents and sisters were killed, I never dared to think that my brother might still be alive. Buk Bol Buk was not at home on that day I went to the market on my own. He had been visiting an uncle and cousins in another village far from ours and was away for several weeks. At least, that's what I remember my parents telling me when he left. So, when John Eibner had told me months before that my parents were dead, I tried not to think about my brother. Had the militia also struck the village where he was? I didn't even know the name of that village. While millions of people had been killed, millions more had survived and had scattered all over Sudan and into other countries. But every Dinka I knew was searching for missing family, with only rare successes. The absence of relatives, the mystery of whether they were alive or dead gnawed at people's lives; unanswered questions about the past made it impossible for some people to move on. Once I got to Khartoum and realized that my story was hardly unique, I knew in my heart that the chances of finding any members of my family alive were slim. Part of me, the survivor in me, never gave up; but another part of me, the person who had seen so much death and had experienced so much cruelty and heard so many more stories of both, assumed everyone from my family was gone. If my brother were alive, how would I find him? And if he were dead, I would have no family left. I would be a true orphan, just one more of "the lost boys." My solution was not to think about him.

But then, in early 2001, I was visiting a friend in Manchester who had a woman from Aweil staying with him, a former SPLA fighter in southern Sudan. When we were introduced she looked at me carefully, and then explained her curiosity. "You look just like someone I know in Sudan, in the SPLA," she said. "He has the same name as you." She explained that this guy was also a Dinka Malwal from West Aweil, about thirty years old. Could it really be my brother? "Buk Bol Buk?" I asked her. She knew him well. Was my brother really still alive?

I told Jesse and Charles, who called John Eibner, asking him to check on the possibility that my brother might be alive. John's group depended on SPLA protection for their slave redemptions, and it would be easy for him to run my brother's name by his SPLA sources on his upcoming trip to Sudan to redeem slaves. It was an exciting prospect, but it would take a while, and I went about my business. And then that morning the voice of the brother I used to call "Buk" came out of my cell phone, saying that he would call back.

He did. "I am happy you are still alive," he said to me.

My own happiness that I was actually talking to my brother filled me up. "After thirteen years of not talking to you, I can't believe that you are still alive," I said to him.

He said that he had actually heard about me before he met John. Aid workers with international organizations routinely delivered food and medicine into the Aweil area, and one of them had heard about this Dinka named "Francis Bok," an escaped slave from Sudan who was trying to get the U.S. government to do something about the war and slavery in his country. Buk Bol wondered if it might be me, his little brother Piol Bol Buk whose Christian name was "Francis." Of course, he did not know that my black market passport makers had turned "Buk" into "Bok." On the phone he said, "I was not sure it was you." And even if he knew it was, how could he reach me? Then John Eibner found him and showed him a picture of me from an American newspaper. He saw the seven-year-old Piol in the grownup Francis Bok.

We spoke for only about five minutes, until we lost the satellite connection. But I wrote him a letter that I was able to get to him through CSI. He wrote back and told me about his wife and kids, and I sent him some money. "I want you to leave the army," I advised him. At the time, government troops were still clashing with SPLA fighters. I had finally found the only surviving member of my immediate family, and I did not want to lose him to a government bullet. I wanted him to get to a nearby country—John suggested

Uganda was safer than Kenya—where he might have a chance of getting UN refugee status and then a visa to the U.S., now that I was living here. Buk Bol explained that it was difficult to leave the army and virtually impossible to get the necessary papers to cross the border with his family. He had to continue fighting against the north.

In my letters, I told him that there are other ways of fighting. Guns are not the only way. I had been in America for only a few years, yet I had already helped change the attitudes of senators and maybe even the President of the United States toward Sudan. I had read about Martin Luther King, Jr. and Ghandi, and I now believed that non-violence could be more effective in confronting the government of Sudan than more shooting and killing. I myself had discovered the power of words—and kept being reminded of how much even one person can accomplish if he tries.

A few weeks after I talked to my brother, I traveled to California. Perry Farrell, the lead singer of Jane's Addiction, had told me in Washington that he wanted me to come to a concert. I figured he was just being polite. But Perry was evidently a man of his word. He had said he wanted to get involved in our cause, and he had. He also called to invite me to appear at concerts he was giving in Santa Barbara and Palm Springs. California for me was Los Angeles—the home of the Los Angeles Lakers. I had never heard of the two cities he mentioned. But I liked the idea of visiting California, and getting there by appearing at a rock concert seemed the very best—and most American—way to go. Perry also promised to promote the AASG's new Web site, iAbolish.com. How could I refuse?

I flew to Los Angeles, visited Perry at his beautiful house, and joined him for an interview at KROQ, one of L.A.'s biggest radio stations. Then I went up to Santa Barbara, a rich, California seaside town and the prettiest place I had ever seen in America. By then I was very comfortable standing in front of a crowd of strangers. I had appeared before audiences of five hundred or so in Washington and Boston. In Santa Barbara, I learned that the concept of a "crowd" was a relative thing. Perry invited me out on stage and introduced me to 20,000 screaming kids. I just stared into the lights and enjoyed their applause. Two days later I was standing in front of 40,000 more kids at an outdoor concert in Palm Springs. This time Perry asked me to talk to the crowd.

"You're all here to have fun tonight," I said. "But I am sorry to tell you that terrible things go on in this world." I told them that "we all know that music is about freedom. But you must all know that there are many people in the world who want to be free like you and to come and participate in something like this that you have the freedom to do, tonight, tomorrow, and the next day. They are people who are dreaming of freedom. You should share your freedom with them."

I explained that if I had been invited to appear at such a concert in 1996, I would not have been able to come, because I was a slave. "Thank God I'm here with you tonight. I want to share my story with you, and I hope those who hear this story will go home and do something about it." To help them, I announced the launch of iAbolish.com, repeating the Web site name at least four times. They clapped and yelled, as only a group of forty thousand teenagers at a rock concert could. I looked out over their faces toward the palm trees silhouetted against the sun setting over the California desert. And I thought about those days back in northern Sudan when I had tried to speak to the other Dinka boys or even to Giemma, and he would tell me to shut up. That night in Palm Springs, I had spoken to forty thousand people, and they listened.

AFTERWORD

THE CONTINUING
STRUGGLE

On Friday, October 18, 2002, Charles Jacobs got a telephone call: "The President would like you and Francis Bok at the White House on Monday to witness the signing of the Sudan Peace Act," said the voice at the other end of the phone.

Charles came out of his office to tell me the news. It would be my second visit to the White House. The previous year, on September 4, a week before the September 11th attacks on the Pentagon and World Trade Center, Charles and I were present for a ceremony on the White House lawn where President George W. Bush announced that he was sending former Senator John Danforth as his special envoy to Sudan to push for peace between the north and south. I did not get to meet President George Bush that day, and I was excited by the prospect of getting another chance to shake hands with the most powerful man in the world. But Charles and I were much more excited by the reason we had been invited to the White House again. For years, AASG had been pressuring Congress, the State Department, and the White House to get the United States to speak out against slavery in Sudan. Washington resisted—until

President Clinton finally denounced "the scourge of slavery" in Sudan on Human Rights Day in 1999. But Clinton was in his last days in office, and the incoming Bush Administration made it clear that they would not be following the previous administration's lead in foreign policy. The AASG and its unusual coalition of religious and political groups on the right and left kept the pressure on Congress.

The result was the Sudan Peace Act, which passed the House and the Senate with overwhelming bipartisan support. It was a great victory for the AASG, and the White House was right to want Charles to be on hand for the President's ceremonial signing of the new legislation. That they wanted me to be present was a true honor—and just one more event in my life that I could never have imagined. Just four years before, I was a refugee from slavery in Africa landing at Kennedy Airport, nervous about beginning a new life in a country whose language I did not know. Now I was heading to Washington as the guest of the President of the United States. The only thing that would be better would be for Giemma Abdullah to know what had happened to his slave, the boy he called "maggot."

On the plane from Boston, Charles and I discussed how we should take advantage of any opportunity we might have to speak to President Bush. Charles guessed that there would be thirty or forty other people in the same room for the ceremony, all trying to catch the President's eye. "We might get a shot at shaking hands with the President," he said. We figured that it would give us a twenty-to-thirty-second opportunity to say something—time for about four sentences. What should we say?

I didn't have to think about it for very long. During my ten years of slavery, I came to believe that no one cared what was happening to me. Otherwise, how could I and those other Dinka boys be working against our will standing in the blistering sun at watering places in northern Sudan? If only we had known that powerful people elsewhere in the world were trying to save us from slavery. I would tell the President about the other kids. Charles and I worked on how I might say that in a few sentences.

We took a taxi from Reagan National Airport. "Take us to the White House, please," Charles told the driver, as we both smiled at each other at how much fun it was to say such a thing. The Pakistani cab driver looked at this American man and his tall, young black associate and asked, "Why are you going to the White House?" "To meet the President," said Charles, and we shared another big grin.

We found a group of people waiting at the White House gate. I recognized some members of Congress I had met before who had been supportive of the AASG efforts to put U.S. pressure on the Sudanese government, including Donald Payne from New Jersey, leader of the Black Caucus and a loyal supporter of the AASG. Joe Madison, the Washington radio talk show host, rushed over to say hello. He, too, was active in antislavery work, and I had appeared on his nationally syndicated radio show several times. No one seemed to mind waiting. We had already given our Social Security numbers and had been warned to bring a photo ID, which we turned over to the White House security guard. As we waited for our security clearance, Charles introduced me to Senator Danforth, a distinguished looking man who was almost as tall as I am. Finally, a security official showed up with White House identification tags that we were to wear around our necks. We were then asked to move through a metal detector and allowed to walk through the grounds toward the West Wing. As we approached the door it seemed to open magically, though it turned out that the magic opener was a young U.S. Marine in full uniform.

Inside, we were directed to the Roosevelt Room, across the hall from the Oval Office where the signing would take place. It was packed with guests taking their seats. Charles and I shot each other a look: Our chances of talking to the President had just gotten very slim. All around the room were Secret Service with wary eyes and wires dangling from their ears, just like in the movies. As we took our seats, Charles pointed out Condoleeza Rice, the President's National Security Advisor, entering the room and taking her seat in the front row. Within a few minutes the President entered, flanked by Secretary of State Colin Powell and John Danforth. The President went to the microphone and made some formal remarks about the war in Sudan and U.S. efforts to bring both sides together, and how important the Sudan Peace Act that he was about to sign would be to peace in Sudan. But he also said something that was very moving for Charles and me: "The act," the American President said, "is designed to address the evils inflicted on the people of Sudan by their government—including the practice of slavery."

The Sudanese government had denied it for decades. Arab students attacked me during my speeches for lying about slavery in Sudan. I had countered that slavery in Sudan was undeniable, and I was evidence. International commissions, including one led by the United States had condemned Sudan for its slave raids, and Senator Danforth had filed a written report to the White House declaring that "The record is clear: The government arms and directs marauding raiders who operate in the south, destroying villages and abducting women and children to serve as chattel servants, herders, and field hands." Now one more President of the United States had confirmed it: Slavery exists in Sudan, and the United States was going to do something about those "evils" that we had suffered. Just hearing Bush say those words made the trip worthwhile.

But it got better. After signing the bill and posing for photographs with the members of Congress who had worked to pass it, President Bush, instead of giving us a wave and heading back across the hall to the Oval Office as we had expected, waded right into the crowd, shaking hands and saying hello to everyone. Charles pushed me into his path, figuring it would be difficult for the President to walk past a six foot six Dinka. I made my way toward him. The President saw me, extended his hand, and I gave him mine—which he held as I thanked him for signing the bill and then quickly said what I had prepared: "If the boys and girls still in slavery could know that today you signed a law to help set them free, their faces would light up in hope. I also want to remind you that you're the first President in one hundred and fifty years to meet with a former slave—myself."

Mr. Bush shook his head at the wonder of that and then said, "It's an honor to help." He was still holding my hand and looked up at me. "You're so tall," he said. "Look at me, and look at you." I laughed, he gave my hand a squeeze and then let go and headed off to shake hands with the other guests, including Charles. I sought out Condoleeza Rice and thanked her for helping us and pushing for the Sudan Peace Act. "You're welcome," she said and smiled at me. I immediately pulled out the camera that Charles and I had brought from the office and asked her if she would mind a picture. She laughed: "As many as you want." I handed the camera to someone nearby and asked him to snap a photo of me and the President's National Security Advisor.

It was a great day for Charles and me—and for the prospect of peace in my country. The Sudan Peace Act states explicitly that the Sudanese regime is committing "genocide" and provides $300 million in U.S. aid for rebuilding the infrastructure in southern Sudan that has been destroyed by decades of war and slave raids. The law requires the Secretary of State to report on war crimes in Sudan, including slavery. It also has some teeth: If the President determines that Khartoum is not negotiating peace in good faith, the law he had just signed gives him the power to vote for a UN arms embargo on Sudan and authorization to ban from the U.S. stock exchanges all oil companies operating in Sudan.

Within two weeks after Bush signed the Sudan Peace Act, Talisman Energy, a Canadian oil company that had been operating in southern Sudan with Khartoum's blessing and getting funding on U.S. stock exchanges, announced that the company was pulling out of Sudan, selling its 25 percent stake in the Greater Nile Petroleum Operating Company for $758 million to an Indian oil and gas firm. It was another triumph for Charles and the AASG. For three years we had been leading a movement that persuaded various institutions, including the Texas Teachers Association, the states of California, New Jersey, and New York, and the world's largest pension fund, TIAA-CREF, to sell their Talisman stock. The AASG argument, which an attorney who sits on the AASG board has put at the center of an ongoing class action suit against Talisman, is that the Canadian oil company's business association with the

Sudanese government and actions around oil fields in southern Sudan have made it an accomplice in genocide.

October 2002, in fact, had turned into an extraordinary month for the AASG. For most of the 1990's, Charles had worked to build a coalition of groups and people who, in some circumstances, would not stand in the same room with each other: the Congressional Black Caucus and the Republican Conservative Jesse Helms, the Urban League and the Salvation Army, the Massachusetts liberal congressman Barney Frank and the founder of the Christian "Moral Majority" Reverend Pat Robertson, not to mention the attorneys Ken Starr and Johnnie Cochran, who made a point of working together to secure the release from jail of antislavery activists who engaged in civil disobedience in front of the Embassy of Sudan. For this partnership, they were called in the press "the Dream Team." This unlikely teamwork expressed better than anything what we stand for: Slavery is not about right and left, but right and wrong. That first day I had met him in Boston, Charles told me that he had been trying to alert Washington to the violence, cruelty, and outright genocide in Sudan. Two million people had been killed and more than 4.4 million displaced, and no one seemed to care. But I could change that, Charles explained, by putting a human face on slavery in Sudan. He kept telling me that I was making a difference. I had had my doubts. That day in the White House my doubts were gone.

Not only had I helped put U.S. pressure on Sudan to stop their war against my people and get the Bush Administration to offer to help rebuild the south if Khartoum really pursued peace, I had helped Charles build what he calls "a new kind of human rights movement created from American civil society—from ordinary Americans on the street to college students, from church and synagogue members to the Salvation Army leadership, African-American activists, and white abolitionists." I had spoken to many of those people personally and reached many more with my interviews in newspapers, on television, and local radio talk shows. When I began speaking around the country few Americans knew about the long civil war in Sudan, never mind the evidence of the raids on villages and the taking of slaves. "I had no idea that such a thing could happen in the world today," is a reaction I heard over and over again. Now many people know. The AASG Web site www.iAbolish.com, which had announced at that rock concert in 2001, now gets 200,000 hits a month. The group has several thousand contributors, and 50,000 activists on the iAbolish e-mail action network.

Another question I often hear is, "Why have the United States, Europe, and the United Nations ignored this killing and slavery in Sudan for so long?" It is a good question, but it is not an easy one to answer. Ever since my days in the refugee camps, where I first realized that the violence and cruelty I had lived through had also turned upside down the lives of millions of other south Sudanese, I had often asked myself the question: "How could the rest of the world let such terrible things happen to my people?" As I learned more about the tragedy of southern Sudan during my stay in Cairo, and then saw the horror stories confirmed in the reports and research that Charles and Jesse had assembled for the AASG, the question persisted: Why were the international groups dedicated to the human rights of Palestinians, Bosnians, and Kosovars so silent when it came to well-documented human rights abuses among the people of south Sudan? Their concern for the rights of oppressed Haitians and for the killings in Somali and Burundi proved that racism was not an issue. So why have they turned away from human rights violations against my people?

The same questions had compelled Charles, as he likes to put it, to give up his day job and become a modern-day abolitionist. Recently, he has come up with his own explanation to this moral blindness to slavery and genocide in Sudan. First, there is the touchy issue of religion. The government of Sudan is a Taliban-like Islamist regime committed to ruling the entire country according to *shariah* law, the strict principles of the Koran. The Dinka people in southern Sudan are either Christians or believe in traditional African religion, and are no more eager to live according to the principles of the Muslim religion than most Americans. Unlike other non-Muslim people who live in Muslim countries—such as the Christian Copts of Egypt and the Jews of Yemen—the south Sudanese rejected a second-class citizenship based on having the "wrong" religion. Khartoum's response has been a jihad against the non-Muslim tribes of the south (and any African Muslim tribes, such as the Nuba, who have supported the rebels). The killing in the south, the refugees, the rapes, slavery, and all the other human rights abuses in Sudan were results of this holy war.

"Who wants to take on religion?" Charles asks. That is one possible reason why the human rights groups have shied away from the tragedy of Sudan. Another reason is what Charles calls "the human rights complex." According to Charles, "the human rights community, composed mostly of compassionate white people, feels a special duty to protest evil done by those who are like 'us.'"

"To predict what the human rights community (and the media) focus on," Charles wrote in the *Boston Globe* October 5, 2002, "look not at the oppressed, look instead at the party seen as the oppressor. Imagine the media coverage and the rights groups' reaction if it were 'whites' enslaving blacks in Sudan." My people, Charles told me many times, would not have been abandoned to slavery and slaughter by the human rights establishment, if Arab Muslims were white Christians or Jews. Having the "right" oppressor would change everything. As evidence, he noted that when the Jordanian government killed thousands of Palestinians who had taken to the streets of Amman in "Black September" of 1970, there was no protest from the international community. When Muslims in Bosnia were killed by white Christians, the West intervened, but when Muslims in Pakistan kill Christian villagers there is only silence. Why this "complex" among people who have devoted their lives to helping others whose rights are being stomped on? "We fear the charge of hypocrisy," Charles explains. "We Westerners, after all, had slaves. We napalmed Vietnam. We live on Native American land. Who are we to judge others? And so we don't stand for all of humanity." The sad result is that the Christian slaves of Sudan, the Muslim slaves of Mauritania, the Tibetans, the Kurds, the Christians in Pakistan, Indonesia, and Egypt become victims twice over—of genocide, religious persecution, and enslavement in their own country, and then of the disinterest of the advanced nations of the West. More south Sudanese have been killed by government troops and militia than the dead in Bosnia, Kosovo, Somalia, Haiti, Rwanda and Burundi *combined*. The human rights abuses in southern Sudan are massive and well documented, and no one claiming to be

an advocate for human rights in the world should be allowed
to ignore such horrors.

The American Anti-Slavery Group is dedicated to making
the universal standard of human rights truly universal. A small
nonprofit organization with a full time staff of six, the AASG
has created a new kind of human rights movement of ordinary
church-goers, college students, and even elementary school
kids who could not believe that slavery still existed in the
world. The passage of the Sudan Peace Act and Talisman's
withdrawal from Sudan has proven how powerful such grass-
roots human rights activism can be. Our success also holds a
powerful political message that was clear to anyone who
looked around the Roosevelt Room in the White House that
morning President Bush signed the Sudan Peace Act. That
room was filled with people from across the political spectrum.
As much fun as it was to shake hands and talk to the President
of the United States, it was equally satisfying to know that I
had helped energize so many different kinds of Americans
who, until they heard about slavery in Sudan, had never given
a moment's thought to the place or to the suffering of millions
of Dinka people.

I never set out to become a public speaker and a human rights
activist. I certainly never imagined myself as a Sudanese politician. But over the past two years I have become all of the above,
while still trying to finish high school. It has been tough to do all
these jobs and still have some fun. Some Sudanese people wonder why I'm doing this, that I'm too young to be a spokesperson
for our cause. Some of my friends wonder why I don't focus on

myself more. But I tell them that we Dinka in the United States have to alert Americans to the suffering in southern Sudan. As a former slave, I have a duty to those who are still slaves. I am proud that God has given me this gift to help other people. The AASG has also given me a national platform to publicize the plight of southern Sudan. Maybe that was why I was able to escape to freedom—to spread the word about slavery.

While AASG has been working with me to help end slavery in Sudan, the organization has always acted against slavery around the world. The group's current challenge is Mauritania, another Islamic nation in the northwest of Africa (south of Morocco and north of Senegal) where Arab and African cultures meet. The same kind of slave raids that happen today to my people took place in Mauritania a thousand years ago. An estimated 100,000 black Africans are enslaved in Mauritania. Born into slavery and the religion of Islam, they have been brought up to believe their purpose in life is to serve their Arab masters faithfully.

Charles made clear that he wanted me to be a voice against slavery not just in Sudan, but everywhere in the world. So, in my speeches I explain that modern slavery is not some strange practice unique to Sudan. Nor does it involve just a few hundred thousand Dinka people who are estimated to be in bondage today in Sudan. Human rights organizations estimate that at least 27 million people in the world are slaves today on nearly every continent. I now point to Mauritania. And to India, the world's largest democracy, with an estimated 10 or more million people living in various forms of slavery. "I speak on behalf of the 27 million who do not have a voice," I tell my audiences. And I will continue to work for their freedom.

But I also have my dream about returning one day to my own country, to the village where I lived with my family. If the Americans can help bring peace to Sudan, I want to return to help rebuild the south. The future political structure of Sudan is now being debated: Some in the south want one, united Sudan; others, arguing that the north and south have two different peoples, believe an independent nation in southern Sudan is the only way to ensure equality and peace. For me, equality is crucial to any political structure in Sudan. Decades of war and Islamization efforts in the south have already destroyed the culture of generations of southern Sudanese. My people and the other non-Muslim tribes of the south must have the same rights to practice their religion and speak their own languages and enjoy their own folkways as the Muslims of the north. If we are to be true citizens of a new Sudan, we cannot settle for second-class status.

Not so long ago, when my ordeal in Sudan was still fresh, the idea that Arab people like Giemma and his armed neighbors could live together peacefully and equally with the Dinka was inconceivable to me. Our religious differences, their racism, their contempt for us as something less than human had created a great wall of hatred between the two peoples that seemed impenetrable to me. But during my stay in the United States, and thanks to my education—especially my readings in American and South African history—I have learned that even great walls of racism can be knocked down. Black people in America had once been enslaved, and even after they were freed and made citizens they were treated as inferior members of society. They worked hard, they struggled for freedom and equality, and laws were changed. Now there are black faces standing next to President Bush, voting in Congress, and sitting on the Supreme Court. That reality was an extraordinary thing for me to discover, a true revelation. And when I read Mark Mathabane's memoir of growing up black in South Africa, the hatred between the whites and blacks there was so familiar to me that the end of apartheid and the integration of South African blacks into that society impressed me as a real possibility for my own country. Like American blacks, the South Africans struggled and fought for their freedom and political equality.

From those historical precedents, I have learned that no one gives a people oppressed for generations their freedom and equality without a struggle. You have to fight for it. But a poor people like the southern Sudanese cannot do it alone. They need help. And that is why my work with the AASG has become so important to me. I am in a position to ask the Americans to help us in our struggle for freedom and equality. And when we achieve those goals, I will go back to Sudan to retrieve what I lost by growing up in the north as slave: the culture and traditions of my people. For me that will be proof of my freedom. Certainly, here in American I am free. But I am still a guest. For me, real freedom is the ability to go back home.

That, I suspect, is still years away. In the meantime I will continue to work with the AASG and for my people. I also have to finish high school, and I want to go to college. It is hard work, but I am still only twenty-four and have plenty of time and energy. And whenever things get tough I think of my father, who told me that I would grow up to do important things in this world. "You are muycharko," he said. "Twelve men."

ACKNOWLEDGMENTS

I would be nothing without my parents, Bol Buk Dal and Adut Al Akok. In seven years they molded me into the man I am today. I miss them every day, and this book is dedicated to them, along with my brother and sisters, Buk, Amin, and Achol—and also my stepmother Marial and my stepbrothers and stepsisters, Buk, Piol, Atong, and Ajok. I had assumed that they too had perished in the militia raid that claimed my parents and sisters. But through contacts in Cairo, I got word that Marial and her children were living in one of the refugee camps outside of Khartoum. We are now in touch, and I dedicate this book to them too. For all the relatives I never got to know, or those whose names I can no longer remember, this book is also for you.

I must also thank my American father, Charles Jacobs, the President of the American Anti-Slavery Group. Charles has supported me, educated me, and stood by me since the day we met. He has devoted his life to helping my people, and on behalf of all the southern Sudanese, I recognize him as an honorary Dinka and a national hero. Charles's example should remind Americans that one righteous person *can* change the world.

This book would not have been possible without the American Anti-Slavery Group and its staff, who have empowered me to speak out and continue to support me every day. Jesse Sage, the Anti-Slavery Group's associate director, tracked me down in Ames, Iowa, and is responsible for transforming me into an activist and public speaker. Jesse is an inspiration to me—even if he mistakenly believes that he can beat me at basketball. Laura Barrett runs the operations of the Anti-Slavery Group with a steady hand, and I always enjoy speaking in public alongside Tommy Calvert, Jr., our Chief of External Operations. Joyce Koo does an incredible job booking my speaking engagements and supporting me as I travel the country, and Liz Gould keeps me going strong. I also want to thank Holland Webb, Emma Reinhardt, Kathleen Kilgore, Vaishali Joglekar, Lexi Dew, David Moore, Sarah Rial, and Christine O'Brien.

Many board members of the Anti-Slavery Group have provided important support over the last three years. Reverend Gerald Bell hosted me at his church when I first came to Boston, welcomed me into his family, and provided spiritual guidance. David Ross introduced me to some of San Francisco's best writers—who first encouraged me to write a book about my life story. Dr. Gloria White Hammond has three times risked her life to provide medical and spiritual aid to my people in southern Sudan. She and her husband Ray are community leaders whom I am honored to work with. Thanks also to the other AASG board members: Rick Mann, Steve Rothstein, George Lewis, and Carey D'Avino, who do so much to support my work. The many student interns of the Anti-Slavery Group have provided me with incredible support. David Rossini guided me around Washington, D.C., and did an amazing job helping to organize the Sudan Campaign. I am particularly grateful to Jay Williams, who has twice visited Sudan to help rescue my people and transported messages between my brother, Buk, and me. I also want to thank Kenny Wang, Chara Itoka, and Rebecca Griffin.

At Christian Solidarity International, John Eibner helped locate my relatives and has done so much to assist my people when the rest of the world abandoned them. Thanks also to John's colleague, Gunnar Wiebalck, who helped connect me with my brother, Buk. I have also met other antislavery activists who inspire me, including fellow survivors Abuk Bak, Moctar Teyeb, Khalifa Hamadi, Jean-Robert Cadet, and Vasantha Gedara. Abdel Nasser Ould Yessa is the foreign secretary of SOS Slaves and an Arab Muslim human rights hero. Born into a family in Mauritania that owned slaves, he rebelled as a teenager to become an abolitionist. I am thankful to have him standing with me in the movement to abolish slavery around the world. Joining us are the many members of the Sudan Coalition, particularly Nina Shea, Joe Madison, Reverend Walter Fauntroy, Rabbi David Saperstein, Faith McDonnell, Jimmy Mulla, Mariam Bell, Michael Horowitz, Reverend T. D. Jakes, Roger Winter, Professor Eric Reeves, Maria Sliwa, Curtis Sliwa, Bishop Macram Gassis, Martha Townley, and everyone else who gave their time for my people.

The literary agent Jim Levine approached me after a speech I gave in New York City and encouraged me to write a book about my life. He has been so supportive and understanding, guiding me through the world of book publishing. Thanks also to his assistant Melynda Bissmeyer. Jim introduced me to the writer Ed Tivnan, who had come to hear me speak at Skidmore

College. Ed and I clicked from the moment we met, and I am grateful for how he has transformed my thoughts onto the page and given me the words to tell my story. The moment I walked into the conference room at St. Martin's Press and met Editor-in-Chief George Witte and his publishing associates, I knew I was home. They listened patiently and respectfully, and seemed genuinely moved by my story and eager about the prospect of turning it into a book. Mr. Witte's editing of our manuscript further helped clarify my story, and his questions and suggestions along the way improved our efforts immensely.

Since I only started school a few years ago, my teachers have contributed enormously to my education. The staff at Jewish Vocational Services and the teachers at Boston Evening Academy have shaped my view of the world and given me important skills. Special thanks to my principals Fred Fontaine and Meg Maccini, to Margie Samp, Ryan Oliver, Michelle Goldin, Sam Del Pina, Mr. Martyn, Jennifer Pastano, and Frank Garcia. As I travel across the country speaking, I visit many schools—and I want to thank all the students I have met over the years who have helped educate me and inspire me to keep going. They have given me hope that this generation of American abolitionists will make a difference. In particular, Barbara Vogel and her students at Highline Elementary School in Aurora, Colorado have done so much for me and my people. And to all the students from elementary school, high school, and college who have written me letters, thank you. I was not able to respond to all of them, but please know that every letter was special to me.

Members of Congress have been very supportive since the first day I visited Washington. Special thanks to Senators Sam Brownback, Jesse Helms, and John Kerry, and Representatives

Tom Tancredo, Donald Payne, Frank Wolf, Eleanor Holmes Norton, Barney Frank, Joe Pitts, and Barbara Lee. Also, my thanks to Condaleeza Rice, Madeleine Albright, and Susan Rice, who all took the time to listen. Many journalists have interviewed me and written about slavery in Sudan. I want to thank in particular Nat Hentoff, who has written about Sudan for so many years; Liz Walker, of WBZ-CBS News, who risked her life to go to Sudan; and to Juan Williams at National Public Radio who patiently interviewed me. Also thanks so much to Perry Farrell, Aaron Cohen, Leigh Vogel, Kevens, Coretta Scott King, Mayor Thomas Menino, Frederick Douglass IV, Al Sharpton, and Russell Simmons. Thanks also to the Boston Celtics for giving me their "Hero Among Us" award, and to Paul Pierce, Antoine Walker, Ed McCarthy, Kenny Anderson, and Jalen Rose.

The southern Sudanese community has kept me alive. Chief Pyo took me in like a son; Franco Majok helped prepare my UN refugee application and changed my life by introducing me to Jesse Sage; Adel, her brother Dau Dau, and everyone else in Ames gave me so much support; Ibrahim Kuol Deng is like a brother to me. Special thanks also to Bona Malwal, who verified my story when I came to Boston and who is a hero to the southern Sudanese, and to Sunia Achol Atak, who means so much to me. So many people helped me in Cairo, Khartoum, and in Southern Sudan and I want to thank all of them. Also, thanks to all the people at Lutheran Social Services, particularly my Fargo social worker Latetia and my sponsor Barry Nelson. Also, thanks to Dr. Dick Bales and his wife, Lynn, who put me up in their home during my early days in Boston.

So many people have helped me that I cannot remember everyone's name. But it doesn't mean that for one minute I forget that I would not be here without their help. To everyone whose name I forget or whom I neglected to include, thank you so much.

Finally, I want to thank God for blessing me and guiding me in the worst of times and the best of times.

ABOUT THE AUTHORS

Francis Bok is twenty-three years old and an associate at the Boston-based American Anti-Slavery Group (AASG). In 2000, he became the first escaped slave to testify before the Senate Committee on Foreign Relations in hearings on Sudan. He speaks throughout the United States, has been featured in *The Boston Globe*, *The Christian Science Monitor*, *The Wall Street Journal*, and *Essence* magazine, and on Black Entertainment Television, and recently met with President George W. Bush at the White House. He lives in Boston. Visit the AASG's Web site at www.iAbolish.com.

Edward Tivnan has collaborated on and is the author of several books. He was a reporter and staff writer for *Time* magazine and helped create ABC's *20/20*. He has appeared on numerous radio and television shows, including on Black Entertainment Television. He lives in Chatham, New York.